REFLECTIONS
FOR **DAILY PRAYER**

REFLECTIONS
FOR **DAILY PRAYER**
PENTECOST TO **TRINITY 12**

12 MAY – 16 AUGUST 2008

ANGELA TILBY
ALICE GOODMAN
CHRISTOPHER JONES
IAN THOMPSON
JANE MAYCOCK
STEPHEN COTTRELL
CHRISTOPHER HERBERT

CHURCH HOUSE
PUBLISHING

Church House Publishing
Church House
Great Smith Street
London SW1P 3AZ

Tel: 020 7898 1451
Fax: 020 7898 1449

ISBN 978 0 7151 4158 8

Published 2008 by Church House Publishing
Copyright © The Archbishops' Council 2008

Designed and typeset by Hugh Hillyard-Parker
Printed by Halstan & Co. Ltd, Amersham, Bucks

Contents

About the authors

Angela Tilby is an Anglican priest in Cambridge and was previously Vice Principal of Westcott House, Cambridge. Prior to that she was a senior producer at the BBC, where she made several acclaimed television programmes and series. She continues to combine parish ministry with her work as a freelance television producer, writer and broadcaster.

Alice Goodman took up the post of Chaplain at Trinity College, Cambridge, in 2006, having served curacies in Redditch and Kidderminster. She combines ministry in college with a number of ongoing writing projects and is well known as the librettist of John Adams' operas *Nixon in China* and *The Death of Klinghoffer*.

Christopher Jones is Policy Adviser for Home Affairs to the Archbishops' Council of the Church of England, specializing in criminal justice and mental health issues. He previously taught systematic theology and served as a college chaplain in Durham and Oxford. He continues to be active in parish ministry and enjoys wrestling with biblical exegesis and interpretation.

Ian Thompson is Dean of Chapel at King's College, Cambridge. Before that he was Dean and Chaplain at Selwyn College and Chaplain at Newnham College, both in Cambridge. He was a Commanding Officer in the Salvation Army for many years before being ordained in 1994.

Jane Maycock recently completed six and a half years as a Diocesan Director of Ordinands in the Diocese of Carlisle, prior to which she served in parishes in Harrow and Kendal. With more time now for writing, she is enjoying exploring the dialogue between literature, theology and spirituality.

Stephen Cottrell is the Bishop of Reading. He is a popular speaker, evangelist, author of *Do Nothing to Change Your Life* and co-author of the *Emmaus: The Way of Faith* series.

Christopher Herbert has been Bishop of St Albans since 1995. He has an interest in, and love for all forms of literature and is a prolific author in his own right. Much of his writing is based on the themes of prayer and spirituality, for both children and adults. Among his best-known books are *Ways into Prayer* and *Pocket Prayers*.

About *Reflections for Daily Prayer*

Based on the *Common Worship Lectionary* readings for Morning Prayer, these daily reflections are designed to refresh and inspire times of personal prayer. The aim is to provide rich, contemporary and engaging insights into Scripture.

Each page lists the lectionary readings for the day with the main psalms for that day highlighted in **bold**. The Collect of the day – either the *Common Worship* collect or the shorter additional collect – is also included.

For those using this book in conjunction with a service of Morning Prayer, the following conventions apply: a psalm printed in parentheses is omitted if it has been used as the opening canticle at that office; a psalm marked with an asterisk may be shortened if desired.

A short reflection is provided on either the Old or New Testament reading. Popular writers, experienced ministers, biblical scholars and theologians will be contributing to this series. They all bring their own emphases, enthusiasms and approaches to biblical interpretation to bear.

Regular users of Morning Prayer and *Time to Pray* (from *Common Worship: Daily Prayer*) and anyone who follows the lectionary for their regular Bible reading will benefit from the rich variety of traditions represented in these stimulating and accessible pieces.

Monday 12 May	Psalms 123, 124, 125, **126**
	Joshua 1
	Luke 9.18-27

Joshua 1

Nothing can disguise the theme of the book of Joshua; it is an account of a Holy War. The children of Israel have been delivered from captivity in Egypt. Now they enter and occupy the Promised Land. God does not save his people from oppression and leave them to fend for themselves; he provides a safe territory with secure borders where they may prosper and be formed as his people. God's purpose is consistent, and he carries it through to the end. As he upheld Moses, so he promises to uphold Joshua. The occupation of territory lived in by others in the name of God raises serious questions today. We rightly abhor violence and find it repulsive to think of God as an invading warrior, wiping out his enemies. But it is important to remember that, from the beginning of the Christian era, these Scriptures of conquest and possession have been interpreted symbolically. That is not to say they do not reflect history, but the main point for Christian readers is to learn what it means for us to be children of God's promise. Not only does God rescue us from the oppression of sin; he also provides opportunities for us to flourish under his protection. What is required of us is faithfulness. Joshua was instructed to meditate on the law; we can deepen our faith through prayer and reflection on Scripture. We may not always feel courageous, but we can always practise courageous living and so prepare ourselves for what John Donne called the 'one equal possession' of eternity.

COLLECT

O Lord, from whom all good things come:
grant to us your humble servants,
that by your holy inspiration
we may think those things that are good,
and by your merciful guiding may perform the same;
through our Lord Jesus Christ,
who is alive and reigns with you,
in the unity of the Holy Spirit,
one God, now and for ever.

Psalms **132**, 133
Joshua 2
Luke 9.28-36

Tuesday 13 May

Joshua 2

Successful campaigns depend on good intelligence, and Israel's conquest of the Promised Land needs careful preparation based on information covertly gathered. But their presence becomes known, and we learn that the news of God's mighty deeds has already reached the inhabitants of the land. The narrator takes care to ensure that we do not feel too sorry for the Canaanites, who, it appears, have already surrendered to fear. Their defeat, he implies, is just. It is harder for us to take that point of view today. We know all too well how the disputes over territory that are still going on in Palestine and Israel are exacerbated by claims of God-given rights to the land.

But there are other aspects of the story that it is perhaps more profitable for us to focus on. Rahab saves the spies. Her role in the story reminds us that God welcomes the outcast and vulnerable, and often gives them a special role in the working out of his purposes. Rahab was blessed because she saw that conquest by the God of Israel could mean not defeat but salvation. She is a forerunner of all those who have responded to a God who cares for the outcast and the marginalized. The Church Father Irenaeus found the shadow of the cross in this passage, suggesting that the scarlet cord that protected Rahab's household was a mystical sign of the blood of Christ shed for us and our salvation.

O Lord, from whom all good things come:
grant to us your humble servants,
that by your holy inspiration
we may think those things that are good,
and by your merciful guiding may perform the same;
through our Lord Jesus Christ,
who is alive and reigns with you,
in the unity of the Holy Spirit,
one God, now and for ever.

COLLECT

3

Wednesday 14 May

Matthias the Apostle

Acts 2.37-end

Today's reading is from the end of the apostle Peter's Pentecost sermon to the Jews in Jerusalem. Peter announces that the last days have come with an outpouring of God's Spirit as a consequence of the resurrection of the crucified Messiah. The response to this from Peter's audience is *compunction*, 'they were cut to the heart' – a memorable phrase, which well expresses the overwhelming sense of need, loss and sinfulness that human beings experience when confronted with the holiness of God. Peter calls his hearers to repent and accept baptism, and with it the same gift of the Spirit that the apostles have received. Our Christian journey involves a continual returning to the sources of our life; a constant reimmersion in the promises of God that will lead us deeper and deeper into both repentance and the joy that follows. St Matthias was chosen by lot to replace Judas. Our baptism draws us into the apostolic mission of Peter and Matthias. We are a Pentecost people. The rather idealized picture of the early Christian community in verses 44 to 47 should not deflate us. Every attempt to live in the Spirit will be a mixture of failures and new beginnings. We can begin again today by asking where the challenge of the gospel causes us to be 'cut to the heart', for that is the point at which we are called to spiritual growth.

COLLECT

Almighty God,
who in the place of the traitor Judas
chose your faithful servant Matthias
to be of the number of the Twelve:
preserve your Church from false apostles
and, by the ministry of faithful pastors and teachers,
keep us steadfast in your truth;
through Jesus Christ your Son our Lord,
who is alive and reigns with you,
in the unity of the Holy Spirit,
one God, now and for ever.

Psalms **143**, 146
Joshua 4.1 – 5.1
Luke 9.51-end

Joshua 4.1 – 5.1

The crossing of the Jordan is told in chapters 3 and 4 as though from different angles, and some of the details are unclear. The point is not so much to give a chronological account of the entry into the Promised Land as to impress the memory of each generation by repetition and recapitulation. The crossing of the Jordan echoes and completes the earlier crossing of the Red Sea. The people who fled Egypt as slaves enter their inheritance as a liberated people. Just as Moses had parted the Red Sea to let them escape, so the Ark with its priestly guardians stops the flow of the Jordan, enabling them to take possession. There is a long and venerable Christian tradition of seeing the crossing of the Jordan as a prefiguring of our journey through death to the Promised Land of heaven – a tradition that begins with the early Christian fathers and survives through to Bunyan's *The Pilgrim's Progress* and the spirituals of the black plantation slaves. Jordan is the 'deep river' that all must cross. 'When I tread the verge of Jordan, bid my anxious cares subside, death of death and hell's destruction, land me safe on Canaan's side.' The fear of death, which is natural for all of us, is for Christians to be seen in the light of Christ's victory over death. He has entered that strange country and made it a promised homeland for us.

O Lord, from whom all good things come:
grant to us your humble servants,
that by your holy inspiration
we may think those things that are good,
and by your merciful guiding may perform the same;
through our Lord Jesus Christ,
who is alive and reigns with you,
in the unity of the Holy Spirit,
one God, now and for ever.

COLLECT

5

Friday 16 May

Joshua 5.2-end

The Israelites have crossed into the Promised Land, but they are not yet God's covenant people. The original generation that passed through the Sinai region rejected God many times on their travels. As a consequence, they were forbidden to enter the land. But the new generation who had entered the land had not yet received the sign of the covenant. Hence the pause in Gilgal for the adult males to be circumcised into the faith of Abraham. From this point they were ritually pure, a holy people, fit to celebrate the Passover. The fact that they entered the Promised Land before they were ritually pure suggests that grace always precedes conversion and commitment. God is always ahead of us, opening the way, inviting us onward. It is only when we know something of the grace of God that we are challenged to active discipleship. That discipleship needs discipline and nourishment. While the Israelites were crossing the Sinai, they were sustained on the provisional manna. Once in the land, they ate the crops of the land. They would need their strength for the Holy War that lay ahead. We, too, if we are to be fit for the Christian struggle against evil and injustice, need to reflect on our baptismal call and to feed on the nourishment of word and sacrament. Otherwise, the immediate task ahead (represented for the Israelites by the man with the drawn sword) will defeat us.

COLLECT

O Lord, from whom all good things come:
grant to us your humble servants,
that by your holy inspiration
we may think those things that are good,
and by your merciful guiding may perform the same;
through our Lord Jesus Christ,
who is alive and reigns with you,
in the unity of the Holy Spirit,
one God, now and for ever.

Psalm 147
Joshua 6.1-20
Luke 10.17-24

Joshua 6.1-20

This is a wonderfully vivid story, although there is no archaeological evidence that would support the dramatic destruction of Jericho as it is described here. What the story points to is the invisible power of God; the fall of the city is a holy act. We tremble at such assumptions. The language of Holy War is one most of us recoil from. Yet we are all ready to rejoice at the downfall of wicked and tyrannical regimes and at the liberation of those who have no rights and no homeland. Unless we are total pacifists (and this is a particular Christian vocation, not given to all), we must allow a place for upheaval and conflict in the purposes of God. The holiness of the siege is emphasized by the fact that the walls fall without violence and that the conquerors are commanded not to indulge in looting. The Israelites are not to begin to behave as if they were a band of thugs; to do so would be to bring destruction on themselves. Meanwhile, the fortified city has a friend of God within it. Joshua insists that Rahab the prostitute is found and protected.

If we are to turn this story into prayer, we might begin by reflecting on the walled, sealed strongholds in our own lives and societies. Could it be that the places where we are most defended are where we are most vulnerable? And that the invisible power of God shatters our defences, not to destroy us but to set us free?

COLLECT

O Lord, from whom all good things come:
grant to us your humble servants,
that by your holy inspiration
we may think those things that are good,
and by your merciful guiding may perform the same;
through our Lord Jesus Christ,
who is alive and reigns with you,
in the unity of the Holy Spirit,
one God, now and for ever.

Monday 19 May

Joshua 7.1-15

'The Israelites broke faith…' The saga of Holy War and conquest takes a new turn as one of the holy warriors is revealed to be a thief. He simply does what conquering armies have always done and removes some of the loot for himself. The act of one man has disastrous consequences for all Israel. What should have been a small-scale assault on Ai turns into a rout. The Israelites are overcome by the same paralysing terror as that to which their Canaanite foes succumbed. Joshua, like Moses before him, pours out his anger and frustration to God. God's response is forthright: Israel is in a state of sin and can only be restored when the perpetrator is found and punished. The assumption is that the belongings of the defeated residents of Jericho are, in some way that is hard for us to grasp, *infected* by God's holiness and can only be safe if they are isolated, destroyed or reserved for use in worship. Holy things are dangerous to God's people. Achan failed to respect the holiness of the spoils and has spread a spiritual infection through the ranks of Israel.

The story is a reminder to us that we are vulnerable to disaster when we fail to respect proper boundaries. Infection spreads in a dirty atmosphere; small acts of dishonesty and acquisitiveness spread a culture where no one's rights are respected.

COLLECT

Almighty and everlasting God,
you have given us your servants grace,
by the confession of a true faith,
to acknowledge the glory of the eternal Trinity
and in the power of the divine majesty to worship the Unity:
keep us steadfast in this faith,
that we may evermore be defended from all adversities;
through Jesus Christ your Son our Lord,
who is alive and reigns with you,
in the unity of the Holy Spirit,
one God, now and for ever.

Psalms **5**, 6 (8)
Joshua 7.16-end
Luke 10.38-end

Joshua 7.16-end

'It is true; I am the one who sinned.' The terrible story of the discovery of Achan and his subsequent execution is made poignant by the very human failing that led to his sin; he saw 'a beautiful mantle from Shinar' along with gold and silver treasure, and he simply could not resist them. Once discovered, most probably through the casting of lots, he is now in the hands of God, and he is urged to give glory and praise to God even as he makes the confession that will condemn him. The unmasking of Achan is God's work; God remains sovereign and free even as he calls Israel into renewed holiness. The one man who has sinned must now die for all so that sins may be forgiven. The wrath of God must be satisfied, or else there is no freedom for his people. Later, the prophet Ezekiel would insist that sin does not spread from person to person; each individual is responsible before God for their own sins. But we can see in Achan's death what would in time become the inclusivity of the gospel. Sinfulness leads to universal death, but righteousness brings life. 'As in Adam all die, even so in Christ shall all be made alive' (I Corinthians 15.21). In our prayers, we might reflect on the mercy of God and his faithfulness, in spite of our tendency to be led astray by the longing for beautiful and desirable things that are not ours to enjoy.

Holy God,
faithful and unchanging:
enlarge our minds with the knowledge of your truth,
and draw us more deeply into the mystery of your love,
that we may truly worship you,
Father, Son and Holy Spirit,
one God, now and for ever.

COLLECT

Wednesday 21 May

Joshua 8.1-29

Joshua's first attempt to defeat the inhabitants of Ai ended in disaster. But Joshua is capable of learning from his mistakes, and, this time, he not only employs his entire fighting force but also sets a trap for the people of Ai, who, on the basis of their last experience, expect the raiders to flee from them. Joshua's forces feign flight, and the armies of Ai rush out to defeat the troops they can see, cutting themselves off from the hidden force who now fall upon the undefended city. The ruthless slaughter of the inhabitants follows, but this time the Lord allows the conquerors to take the livestock of the city and some booty for themselves. The king of Ai is hanged according to the prescriptions of the law, a law that would be followed when Christ was crucified – no body could be left in the place of execution after sunset. The slaughter of the innocent is terrible for us to read, but perhaps in our own time we should reflect on what should be a Christian response to those who have no homeland. Are we able to welcome economic refugees, migrants, asylum-seekers and all those displaced persons in our world in desperate need of security and freedom? Joshua and his forces took what had been promised to them with violence and terror. How good are we at making space for the strangers within our borders?

COLLECT

Almighty and everlasting God,
you have given us your servants grace,
by the confession of a true faith,
to acknowledge the glory of the eternal Trinity
and in the power of the divine majesty to worship the Unity:
keep us steadfast in this faith,
that we may evermore be defended from all adversities;
through Jesus Christ your Son our Lord,
who is alive and reigns with you,
in the unity of the Holy Spirit,
one God, now and for ever.

Psalm 147
Deuteronomy 8.2-16
1 Corinthians 10.1-17

Day of Thanksgiving for the Institution of Holy Communion (Corpus Christi)

1 Corinthians 10.1-17

Paul struggles in this passage to explain the implications of being part of the body of Christ. He takes an example from the Exodus story. The Israelites all participated in the same saving events, and yet those who denied their salvation by acting immorally were poisoned by serpents. Their fate warns us of the seriousness of Christian participation in the body of Christ. In this sense, the Israelites are our spiritual ancestors. They were 'baptized into Moses' and became one body; they 'ate the same spiritual food, and all drank the same spiritual drink'. As we prepare ourselves for participation in the sacrament of the Eucharist, we should always remember that what we receive is holy, and makes us holy: 'God's holy gifts for God's holy people.' Paul implies here, as elsewhere, that we can actually be harmed by participating in Holy Communion carelessly or casually. It tears us apart to belong to Christ sacramentally while denying him in the rest of our lives. Important though Paul's warnings are, they are only one side of the picture. A reluctance to take the risk of communicating unworthily has kept many away from the sacramental life. The cup we share is a cup of blessing, and the body is intended to strengthen us for service. We are not invited to be hurt; we come to the Lord's table not because we are worthy, but because we are unworthy.

COLLECT

Lord Jesus Christ,
we thank you that in this wonderful sacrament
you have given us the memorial of your passion:
grant us so to reverence the sacred mysteries
of your body and blood
that we may know within ourselves
and show forth in our lives
the fruits of your redemption;
for you are alive and reign with the Father
in the unity of the Holy Spirit,
one God, now and for ever.

11

Friday 23 May

Joshua 9.3-26

In today's reading, we see how the cunning war strategy of Joshua is met by cunning. The Gibeonites take desperate measures to prevent their own annihilation, and they succeed, though at the cost of their own freedom; the Gibeonites would remain menial workers in the later Jerusalem temple. Texts like this, detached from their context, have been interpreted to imply that God has predestined particular races or classes to have slave status, as 'hewers of wood and drawers of water'. But there is no justification for such an interpretation. What is more important is the fact that the Israelites were faithful to the treaty that they made with the Gibeonites. Though they had been taken in by a clever ruse, they could not go back on the peace they had sworn without incurring God's wrath. Slowly, painfully, God forms his people in habits of faithfulness. We, too, need to learn to grow in faithfulness by learning to depend on the long-suffering mercy of God. The promises that we have made – as Christians, as children and parents, as spouses, and even in the ordinary trust invested in us in the workplace – call us back again and again to the one who calls, who is faithful (1 Thessalonians 5.24).

COLLECT

Almighty and everlasting God,
you have given us your servants grace,
by the confession of a true faith,
to acknowledge the glory of the eternal Trinity
and in the power of the divine majesty to worship the Unity:
keep us steadfast in this faith,
that we may evermore be defended from all adversities;
through Jesus Christ your Son our Lord,
who is alive and reigns with you,
in the unity of the Holy Spirit,
one God, now and for ever.

Psalms 20, 21, **23**
Joshua 10.1-15
Luke 11.37-end

Joshua 10.1-15

The faithfulness of the Israelites to the conquered Gibeonites is put to the test by the alliance of the five kings against Gibeon. Joshua responds to the threat at once and organizes a surprise march from Gilgal. The description of the battle is extraordinary in that it involves the Lord being portrayed, quite literally, as a warrior, hurling hailstones from heaven upon the enemy troops. However disturbing the imagery, the point here is to emphasize God's loyalty to those who have made peace with his people. That loyalty takes precedence over the laws of nature; the sun stands still and the moon stops. A whole extra day passes for the victory to be completed. This is the poetry of faith, and we should not feel compelled to interpret it literally. In describing Christ's victory on the cross, the Gospel-writers speak of the sun going into darkness at the climax of the passion. The Lord of history is also the Lord of nature, and the great deeds of our salvation are celebrated symbolically through the portrayal of dramatic events in the natural world. The defeat of the five kings reminds us that even the best-established states are vulnerable to the tide of change; human domination is never for ever. When we pray for the world in its long-standing conflicts and wars, we do so with a longing for the peace that only God can bring; human violence and hatred can only be defeated by Christ-like deeds of sacrificial love.

Holy God,
faithful and unchanging:
enlarge our minds with the knowledge of your truth,
and draw us more deeply into the mystery of your love,
that we may truly worship you,
Father, Son and Holy Spirit,
one God, now and for ever.

COLLECT

Monday 26 May

Luke 12.1-12

There are thousands of people here, pushing near to catch what Jesus is saying. They want to be near him, to see him, to touch him if they can. Above all, though, they want to hear his words. The people have become a crowd, and, in the midst of the crowd, people are being trampled. Not deliberately trampled, you understand. Haplessly, helplessly trampled, as happens when a crowd becomes something more and less than the individual people within it. You've seen the pictures: the lost shoe, the torn book, someone crouched in the dust, face contorted with grief.

But Jesus isn't speaking to the crowd. At this moment, his words are for his disciples. He's speaking clearly and intimately about fear: the fear of exposure and the terror of death. For each of us, as for the disciples, these are familiar fears, ones we hug to ourselves and are ashamed to speak of. The yeast of the hypocrites is the fear of being seen in the nakedness of their human frailty. What is my inspiration? What moves me to act? I see a face in the crowd and, for a moment, cherish it. God has numbered every hair, seen into every heart, and grieves over all who fell. Let that sink in: knowing it will teach you what to say.

COLLECT

O God,
the strength of all those who put their trust in you,
mercifully accept our prayers
and, because through the weakness of our mortal nature
we can do no good thing without you,
grant us the help of your grace,
that in the keeping of your commandments
we may please you both in will and deed;
through Jesus Christ your Son our Lord,
who is alive and reigns with you,
in the unity of the Holy Spirit,
one God, now and for ever.

Psalms 32, **36**
Joshua 21.43 – 22.8
Luke 12.13-21

Tuesday 27 May

Luke 12.13-21

It seems reasonable enough. If Jesus is not judge, then who is? Certainly, one of the primary duties of a rabbi is to arbitrate in cases like this man's: to look at the situation between these brothers in the light of Torah and say how the inheritance should be divided. Moses, after all, had seen fit to bring the matter of the inheritance of the daughters of Zelophehad before the Lord, and the Lord adjudicated in their favour. The story takes up fully half of the twenty-eighth chapter of the Book of Numbers. If Jesus is not going to do this kind of work, then what work is he doing? He is doing the work of setting us right with God with a view towards the last things.

'Build thee more stately mansions, O my soul!', says the American poet Oliver Wendell Holmes in a solemn riff on this parable. But the soul is restless in any mansion of its own building and cannot relax even when surrounded with a mountain of goods. Greed, being rooted in insecurity, is insatiable. 'Friend,' says Jesus ironically. 'Soul,' says the rich man to himself. 'Consumer,' says the world, redefining the man. 'You fool!' says God, 'Your life, your rest, your riches, your inheritance are nothing if they are not in me.'

God of truth,
help us to keep your law of love
and to walk in ways of wisdom,
that we may find true life
in Jesus Christ your Son.

COLLECT

15

Wednesday 28 May

Psalm **34**
Joshua 22.9-end
Luke 12.22-31

Luke 12.22-31

Sometimes, just for a moment, it looks as if Jesus is giving us a clear instruction that we can act upon. For a moment, as now while he speaks to his disciples, everything becomes simple. We have a rule to follow: 'Do not worry about your life.' As I write this, I am half-listening to the voice of the great Sufi singer Nusrat Fateh Ali Khan improvising the praises of the One God so felicitously that, for a moment, I actually do stop worrying about my life. Then the continuity announcer cuts in. It is time for the news. Every briefing, every correspondent excites a fresh sense of impending disaster. The grasshopper sings through the summer and dies when it turns cold. I am *homo anxius*, human because I look into the future with fear. How can I *not* worry about my life? It is an inexplicable mystery that flowers are perennial, that the ravens that fed Elijah find something for themselves. And there I pause. In Jesus' humanity is the promise – the guarantee even – that anxiety is not intrinsic to our humanity. It is part of the fallenness of the world, a thorn in my flesh, but not part of my self.

COLLECT

O God,
the strength of all those who put their trust in you,
mercifully accept our prayers
and, because through the weakness of our mortal nature
we can do no good thing without you,
grant us the help of your grace,
that in the keeping of your commandments
we may please you both in will and deed;
through Jesus Christ your Son our Lord,
who is alive and reigns with you,
in the unity of the Holy Spirit,
one God, now and for ever.

Psalm 37*
Joshua 23
Luke 12.32-40

Luke 12.32-40

'Be dressed for action.' The Greek word translated here means something like 'let your belts be cinched up'; some translations have that splendid expression 'gird your loins'. There's an echo here from the Lord's commandments to Moses concerning the first Passover sacrifice: 'This is how you shall eat it: your loins girded, your sandals on your feet, and your staff in your hand; and you shall eat it hurriedly' (Exodus 12.11). You wouldn't eat the Passover that way now. As any Jewish child will tell you, the Passover meal is eaten reclining, on comfortable chairs. And the reason? 'We were slaves, and the Lord delivered us.' Jesus, celebrating the Passover in Jerusalem, would himself have reclined. We, along with Jesus and the children of Israel, cultivate the memory of having been redeemed. It is the only thing that holds us together; it is our way of realizing we are free. But Jesus takes us back to that original last night of slavery and exile. Be dressed for action, Jesus says, and, when the Lord comes, he will kilt up his tunic and serve as you serve now. 'Attention', according to the seventeenth-century philosopher Nicolas Malebranche, 'is the natural prayer of the soul.' We pay attention to that which we desire. If what you desire is the kingdom of God, it isn't yet time for the comfortable chairs.

God of truth,
help us to keep your law of love
and to walk in ways of wisdom,
that we may find true life
in Jesus Christ your Son.

COLLECT

Friday 30 May

Luke 12.41-48

It gets harder as you go along. The people who say 'Your faith must be such a consolation at a time like this' or 'It's easy for you – you believe' simply do not have a clue. That bunch of keys at your waist: one of them opens the chest with the silver, one of them unlocks the stable door; two of the others are for the pantry and the wine cellar. Men and women alike, the slaves look to you. You have your favourites among them: the hard-working and the attractive. Some of them, though, are infuriating. What it is to be given dominion over a world! Peter, asking his question, already has a sense of what Jesus will say. As you wait for your master's return; as you wait, attentive to your trust, conscious of each one who looks to you, you will be lonely and you will be tempted. The greater the trust, the harder the waiting and the worse the temptation. The more you know, the closer you are, the darker the night is for you, and the stricter the account. Look at pictures of the saints. How do you tell which one is Peter? He is the one with the keys; some artists paint him as an old man in tears.

COLLECT

O God,
the strength of all those who put their trust in you,
mercifully accept our prayers
and, because through the weakness of our mortal nature
we can do no good thing without you,
grant us the help of your grace,
that in the keeping of your commandments
we may please you both in will and deed;
through Jesus Christ your Son our Lord,
who is alive and reigns with you,
in the unity of the Holy Spirit,
one God, now and for ever.

Psalms 85, 150
1 Samuel 2.1-10
Mark 3.31-35

The Visit of the Blessed Virgin Mary
to Elizabeth

Mark 3.31-35

'Blessed are you among women,' Elizabeth cries, 'and blessed is the fruit of your womb.' On the day when the Church commemorates the visit of the Blessed Virgin Mary to Elizabeth, this passage from Mark's Gospel pulls you up short. Queen of Heaven, is she? Mother of God? Do you want to call her 'the Immaculate Conception?' Then you had better be able to think of her also in terms of that anonymous 'whoever'.

At the heart of Christianity is the scandal of particularity. The Word was made not just flesh, but this flesh at this time in the history of this people: Jesus of Nazareth, King of the Jews. We bless every moment, word and person who brought our salvation. Therefore to say, as Jesus says, 'whoever wants to be first must be last of all and servant of all', 'whoever welcomes one such child in my name welcomes me', 'whoever welcomes me welcomes not me but the one who sent me', is not to denigrate Mary, but to raise up any and all who do God's will. It's the old nature versus nurture conundrum, turned a new way. Whoever is reborn in Christ is a new creation. Whoever does the will of God is an adopted child of the Father, co-heir with Christ. It's not simply nature, then, or nurture. The Word was made flesh, but flesh was not the last word.

Mighty God,
by whose grace Elizabeth rejoiced with Mary
and greeted her as the mother of the Lord:
look with favour on your lowly servants
that, with Mary, we may magnify your holy name
and rejoice to acclaim her Son our Saviour,
who is alive and reigns with you,
in the unity of the Holy Spirit,
one God, now and for ever.

COLLECT

19

Monday 2 June

Luke 13.1-9

'I believe the Bible is in part to blame,' wrote the great twentieth-century gardener Christopher Lloyd. He was remembering the fig trees he had seen, 'starved into unproductiveness, simply because the owner has heard so often about the barren fig whose roots were unrestricted'. Among these fig trees, Lloyd conflates two: the barren fig tree in the eleventh chapter of Mark and the one here. Being a gardener, he imagines them clearly and loves them even in their barrenness: 'beautiful in winter sunshine with the tracery of their shadows cast on the wall behind'. When should we expect our trees to bear fruit? The owner of the vineyard comes back year after year, mouth watering, and finds nothing. A hungry man can take no joy in the shadows of barren trees. The fruit in question here is not so much the fig – a fig for that! – as repentance. You walked away from the fallen tower brushing ash off your coat; do you think that makes you better than those who lie in the dust? Where are your roots? You have been given a little more time, that is all. Time to repent, to turn towards the source of all fruitfulness. On Ash Wednesday, we read the book of Joel, in whose vision God sees the tear-stained face of his people, and, in response, 'the fig tree and the vine give their full yield'.

COLLECT

Lord, you have taught us
that all our doings without love are nothing worth:
send your Holy Spirit
and pour into our hearts that most excellent gift of love,
the true bond of peace and of all virtues,
without which whoever lives is counted dead before you.
Grant this for your only Son Jesus Christ's sake,
who is alive and reigns with you,
in the unity of the Holy Spirit,
one God, now and for ever.

Psalms **48**, 52
Judges 4.1-23
Luke 13.10-21

Luke 13.10-21

The leader of the synagogue was quite right. Or at least he was not wrong. About the Sabbath, that is. In Exodus and Deuteronomy, the law is established: 'Remember the Sabbath day, and keep it holy'. The Sabbath comes as a coda to the story of Creation: 'And on the seventh day God finished the work that he had done, and he rested on the seventh day from all the work that he had done. So God blessed the seventh day and hallowed it, because on it God rested from all the work that he had done in creation' (Genesis 2.1-3). On the Sabbath, if you are a religious Jew or an old-fashioned Christian, you may not create and you may not destroy. You are free to rest. Rest includes prayer. It includes sleep. It includes church. What else it might include has been a matter of debate among Jews and Christians for millennia. May I see the doctor? What is healing but making new? Healing is a sign that God is not yet finished with us; Creation is not yet done. When we say 'God saw everything that he had made, and indeed, it was very good', what we say is born of faith and hope, as well as commemoration. The work goes on; it hangs in the balance till kingdom come.

Faithful Creator,
whose mercy never fails:
deepen our faithfulness to you
and to your living Word,
Jesus Christ our Lord.

COLLECT

21

Wednesday 4 June

Luke 13.22-end

This passage does not come from a historical novel, nor is it reportage. Everything here was written in the light of the resurrection. 'Going to Jerusalem' is Gospel code for going towards the cross. That is the road Jesus is on, and here he seems to need to cover every yard of it. Leaving the road, evading Herod, is to leave the way of the Father's will. Compare the advice given by an older pilgrim to a younger one in *The Scale of Perfection,* Walter Hilton's fourteenth-century devotional treatise: 'What so thou hearest or seest or feelest that should let* thee in thy way, abide not with it wilfully, tarry not for it restfully, behold it not, like it not, dread it not; but aye go forth in thy way, and think that thou wouldest be at Jerusalem.' There's more than a touch of quietism, of passive disengagement, in Hilton. As Jesus walks towards Jerusalem, however, his eyes catch the eyes of the villagers; he sees people coming from every point of the compass. At the tips of his fingers, he senses the brute actuality of the world. It's a world about to be turned upside down, with both doom and unexpected hope for all. Even Herod can be healed. Never distracted, never blinkered, Jesus walks among his people as he walks towards his death.

*let = obstruct

COLLECT

Lord, you have taught us
that all our doings without love are nothing worth:
send your Holy Spirit
and pour into our hearts that most excellent gift of love,
the true bond of peace and of all virtues,
without which whoever lives is counted dead before you.
Grant this for your only Son Jesus Christ's sake,
who is alive and reigns with you,
in the unity of the Holy Spirit,
one God, now and for ever.

Psalms 56, **57** (63*)
Judges 6.1-24
Luke 14.1-11

Luke 14.1-11

The thing about Jesus that sticks in the craw was not that he ate and drank with publicans and sinners, but that he also ate and drank with scribes and Pharisees.

I don't know about you, but I'm fond of thinking of him as the companion of tax-collectors and prostitutes, people the Church likes to refer to as 'the marginalized'. Raffish people. Snappers-up of unconsidered trifles. Angels with dirty faces. It takes a wrench of the Christian imagination to recognize Jesus as the welcome guest at the Pharisee's Sabbath meal, eating, drinking, arguing, being argued with, singing grace and embracing at the door. When we imagine the wedding banquet of the Lamb, we seem to have trouble with the seating plan. Who will sit beside the Lord? Who will take the high place, and who will take the low? Who will be asked to move up higher? Who will dip their bread in his dish? Is it the case that I can only find a place for myself if there are other people, sinners or Pharisees, who are not allowed at the table at all? Am I afraid of being asked to give up my place? All these people have been invited; so have I. And we are none of us better than we should be.

Faithful Creator,
whose mercy never fails:
deepen our faithfulness to you
and to your living Word,
Jesus Christ our Lord.

COLLECT

23

Friday 6 June

Psalms **51**, 54
Judges 6.25-end
Luke 14.12-24

Luke 14.12-24

The poor, the crippled, the lame and the blind. Pity them in their powerlessness. If you graciously invite them to your luncheon (at once a vision presents itself of place cards and floral centrepieces), they cannot reciprocate. You're never going to get an invitation to *their* luncheon. Furthermore, they have no excuse to decline your invitation. The poor man cannot buy a piece of land. The blind man cannot go out to see it. The crippled and the lame are incapable of trying out a new yoke of oxen. For the purposes of this parable, the poor, the crippled, the lame and the blind are also the unmarriageable. Buying land, trying oxen, marriage and the begetting of children: each signifies an investment in the world. Before the children of Israel entered into battle, an official was to come before the ranks of the army and send home all those who had such matters to attend to (Deuteronomy 20.5-7). Others fought while these married and dedicated their houses, precisely because such investments in the life of the world were what they were fighting for. These excuses cut no ice with the host in the parable. His tables are set and his luncheon prepared. His servant will bring in those of us who, try as we might, cannot avoid him. We are the walking wounded: poor, crippled, blind and lame.

Lord, you have taught us
that all our doings without love are nothing worth:
send your Holy Spirit
and pour into our hearts that most excellent gift of love,
the true bond of peace and of all virtues,
without which whoever lives is counted dead before you.
Grant this for your only Son Jesus Christ's sake,
who is alive and reigns with you,
in the unity of the Holy Spirit,
one God, now and for ever.

Psalm **68**
Judges 7
Luke 14.25-end

Luke 14.25-end

When people refer to the hard sayings of Jesus, this is the one they most often have in mind. And within this saying, it is the part about hating father and mother, wife and children, brothers and sisters that appals. Is Jesus truly asking me to hate (the Greek is *misein*: hate is what it means) my parents who gave me life and first showed me love, who taught me the very expressions of my face? My spouse, the flesh of my flesh, along with my children, who carry my name and my face forward into time? My siblings, who share all my memories? 'Yes, and even life itself.' If there were fine print on the bottom of your certificate of baptism, this is what it would say. This is the cost of discipleship spread over a lifetime, with interest. Who makes up this massive crowd? Some of us are looking for a miracle: healing for myself or for my child. Some of us want to make sense of our lives. Some of us know a good show when we see it. Even the disciples are hoping for something: a Messiah who calls them by name. What matters to Jesus is the kingdom of God. Everything flows from that source. There are thousands of people here, pushing near to hear what Jesus is saying. He is walking upstream, against the current.

Faithful Creator,
whose mercy never fails:
deepen our faithfulness to you
and to your living Word,
Jesus Christ our Lord.

COLLECT

25

Monday 9 June

Psalm 71
Judges 8.22-end
Luke 15.1-10

Luke 15.1-10

What do we do when we lose something? Both these parables demonstrate an intense effort to regain something highly valued. The painstaking searches of the shepherd and the woman mirror God's active compassion for every person who runs into trouble. The faithful Creator is not indifferent, but seeks out with persistence and determination those who have strayed, to restore them to his loving care.

The joy of finding is highlighted as the crucial point of both parables. The solitary rejoicing of the shepherd on the way home and the celebration of the woman with her friends and neighbours are comparable with the joy of God over sinners who repent. The keynote is not the condition of repentance but the irrepressible desire of God for people to return to him and his overflowing gladness when they do.

Jesus contrasts sharply the judgemental attitude of his Pharisee critics with the welcoming outreach of God. Is God's covenant community a mutual admiration society for the virtuous or a place of refuge for failures? Every Christian and every church ought to ask themselves whether they genuinely share the divine passion to go out to those who have lost their way and the divine happiness when the lost return.

COLLECT

Almighty God,
you have broken the tyranny of sin
and have sent the Spirit of your Son into our hearts
    whereby we call you Father:
give us grace to dedicate our freedom to your service,
that we and all creation may be brought
    to the glorious liberty of the children of God;
through Jesus Christ your Son our Lord,
who is alive and reigns with you,
in the unity of the Holy Spirit,
one God, now and for ever.

Psalm **73**
Judges 9.1-21
Luke 15.11-end

Luke 15.11-end

The father is the central character of this story. The younger son's initiative in leaving home may seem to leave his father in a passive role, but, as the disastrous nature of his chosen way of life unfolds, it is the memory of his father's care that reasserts itself. His repentance, 'coming to himself', is a turning from failure only because it is a turning to the source of hope.

Beyond his hopes, the 'waiting father' runs to meet him on his return. The prodigal's carefully rehearsed speech is held up by the paternal embrace and cut short by the announcement of a homecoming party. Repentance is the grateful and humble acceptance of God's merciful acceptance of us – not a way of pacifying God by self-abasement.

The grumbling Pharisees are now represented by the reaction of the elder son, but it is too easy to dismiss his protests as mere jealousy or self-righteousness. Jesus confronts us with both the unexpected good news and the radical unfairness of God's free love. As we struggle with this gift, we may recognize something of both sons in ourselves. It is as we are met by Jesus, the incarnate Son who himself bore the burden of human conflict and alienation, that we find our way home to the Father and to our estranged brothers and sisters.

God our saviour,
look on this wounded world
in pity and in power;
hold us fast to your promises of peace
won for us by your Son,
our Saviour Jesus Christ.

COLLECT

Wednesday 11 June

Barnabas the Apostle

Psalms 100, 101, 117
Jeremiah 9.23,24
Acts 4.32-37

Acts 4.32-37

Wealth and poverty are major concerns of Luke the evangelist. Hence, it is fitting that today's interruption of the course of readings replaces the parable of the unjust steward by Luke's account in Acts of the faithful apostle Barnabas.

Barnabas first appears as part of a bold development in the life of the Jerusalem church. Some of its members were moved to sell their land and property, and hand over the proceeds for redistribution among the needy. One Joseph, a Cypriot Jew, was prominent among them, his personal qualities attested by the nickname he earned, 'son of encouragement'.

Barnabas later played a major role in overcoming the apostles' suspicion of the convert Saul. He was a trusted ambassador between the churches of Jerusalem and Antioch and a leader of the mission to the gentiles. Even his fierce quarrel with Paul was sparked by his generous attitude to their colleague Mark. His open-heartedness in selling his field for the benefit of others was the first step in an expanding and fruitful ministry. 'He was a good man, full of the Holy Spirit and of faith' (Acts 11.24) – entrusted with great tasks because he was initially faithful in small ones. The Church sorely needs open-hearted, bridge-building sons and daughters of encouragement.

COLLECT

Bountiful God, giver of all gifts,
who poured your Spirit upon your servant Barnabas
and gave him grace to encourage others:
help us, by his example,
to be generous in our judgements
and unselfish in our service;
through Jesus Christ your Son our Lord,
who is alive and reigns with you,
in the unity of the Holy Spirit,
one God, now and for ever.

Luke 16.19-end

Why should we care for the poor? This haunting passage begins with a Jewish version of an ancient folk-tale about the reversal of fortunes in the afterlife. It fulfils the blessings and woes pronounced by Jesus in Luke 6.20-21 and 24-25 and demolishes a theology held by many Jews then and by some Christians today, that wealth is a clear sign of divine favour.

Instead, it is apparent that the rich man failed to use his wealth to help a starving and sick fellow human being on his own doorstep. Profoundly shocked to find himself thirsting in the torment of Hades, he is desperate to save his brothers from a like fate.

The second part of the story takes a provocative twist as Abraham confounds the rich man's assumptions about human motivation. If the consciences of the prosperous are hardened against biblical teaching on obligations to the poor, they will not be softened by warnings about hellfire – or even by a miraculous resurrection. Awareness of God's justice and compassion, with its potential to disturb and transform us, must be received on its own terms. Jesus, fulfilling the law and the prophets, draws us away from self-absorption and calls us to respond to human need because love demands it.

COLLECT

Almighty God,
you have broken the tyranny of sin
and have sent the Spirit of your Son into our hearts
whereby we call you Father:
give us grace to dedicate our freedom to your service,
that we and all creation may be brought
to the glorious liberty of the children of God;
through Jesus Christ your Son our Lord,
who is alive and reigns with you,
in the unity of the Holy Spirit,
one God, now and for ever.

Friday 13 June

Psalm **55**
Judges 11.29-end
Luke 17.1-10

Luke 17.1-10

Jesus prepared his disciples for the demands of life together. In any group, there are various kinds of susceptibility to temptation. So he warns us to be aware of others' weaknesses and not to put difficulties in their way. We are responsible not only for ourselves but also for helping our fellow Christians to avoid sin.

Mutual responsibility is also required to handle disputes in the life of Christian communities. Jesus counsels his followers not to nurse grievances, but to discuss them directly and to resolve them by seeking repentance and forgiveness – a process of conciliation that is to be pursued without limit, as many times as it may be needed.

The disciples (here 'apostles') ask for greater faith. Jesus replies with a picturesque challenge to contemplate the impossible – the sycamore tree being especially resistant to uprooting – and to believe that God can do it. In any difficult situation, even a glimmer of faith opens us to God's power to act beyond normal expectations.

However, Jesus warns against any notion that faithful service gives us rights over against God. The description 'unworthy servants' does not negate the value of our actions, but reminds us that we are always indebted to God's goodness, and not vice versa.

COLLECT

Almighty God,
you have broken the tyranny of sin
and have sent the Spirit of your Son into our hearts
    whereby we call you Father:
give us grace to dedicate our freedom to your service,
that we and all creation may be brought
    to the glorious liberty of the children of God;
through Jesus Christ your Son our Lord,
who is alive and reigns with you,
in the unity of the Holy Spirit,
one God, now and for ever.

Psalms **76**, 79
Judges 12.1-7
Luke 17.11-19

Luke 17.11-19

In recounting Jesus' healing of lepers, Luke underlines the love of God for social and religious outcasts, isolated and stigmatized by their ritual uncleanness. Given the setting, near the region of Samaria, it is likely that he focuses on the Samaritan leper (a twofold outsider) to anticipate the coming of salvation to the gentiles. Here as elsewhere, Jesus attends sympathetically to people on the edge and draws them back into society.

It has often been asked why Jesus criticizes the nine lepers for obeying his command – to go and show themselves to the priests, as required by Leviticus to certify a cure. The point is rather that the Samaritan is commended for seeing the deeper significance of what had happened to him, returning to thank Jesus and praise God for it.

The verb 'made well' also means 'saved'. There may be an allusion in this incident to the historical precedent of Naaman the Syrian, who was both healed of leprosy and converted to worship of the God of Israel (2 Kings 5.1-14). The action of the Samaritan is a response of faith to the breaking in of God's kingdom. Sometimes the receptive outsider grasps the God-given meaning of events that jaded insiders miss or take for granted.

COLLECT

God our saviour,
look on this wounded world
in pity and in power;
hold us fast to your promises of peace
won for us by your Son,
our Saviour Jesus Christ.

Monday 16 June

Psalms **80**, 82
Judges 13.1-24
Luke 17.20-end

Luke 17.20-end

The coming of God's kingdom has always been difficult to understand. Jesus tells the Pharisees that the kingdom does not come with observable signs but is in their midst. He goes on to speak enigmatically of the future coming of the Son of Man. How are these two sets of sayings related?

The reply to the Pharisees implies that the kingdom is present in Jesus' words and deeds, to be perceived by faith. This is confirmed by the declaration that the Son of Man must undergo suffering and rejection before returning. The biblical stories of Noah and Lot are then cited to foreshadow a final crisis of universal judgement, which only the prepared and alert will survive. The abruptness of the crisis will cut across the activities of everyday life, and it will be as inevitable in its impact as the gathering of vultures round a corpse.

Somehow our Christian vision must remain bifocal, holding together the reign of God as we currently experience it and the mystery of its promised fulfilment, which colours the present with both encouragement and warning. What is beyond dispute is that the character of the kingdom is defined by Jesus himself, and that the urgency of responding to its coming is ever-present.

COLLECT

O God, the protector of all who trust in you,
without whom nothing is strong, nothing is holy:
increase and multiply upon us your mercy;
that with you as our ruler and guide
we may so pass through things temporal
that we lose not our hold on things eternal;
grant this, heavenly Father,
for our Lord Jesus Christ's sake,
who is alive and reigns with you,
in the unity of the Holy Spirit,
one God, now and for ever.

Psalms 87, **89.1-18**
Judges 14
Luke 18.1-14

Luke 18.1-14

The main point of the first parable – that we should persist in prayer despite discouragement – is established in a manner similar to the parable of the neighbour in need (Luke 11.5-8). The judge is indifferent to both God and human opinion; only persistence to the point of nuisance can prevail. If such a judge gives way to an unrelenting petitioner, how much more will a righteous and gracious God heed his chosen ones as they pray for vindication in the face of opposition?

The second parable sums up the gospel message in a scandalous verdict on two utterly different people at prayer. The upright Pharisee is proud, contemptuous and self-centred. There is no implication that he is untruthful in rehearsing his spiritual and moral strengths. However, he lacks the essential disposition, of self-abandonment to the divine mercy, shown by the despised tax-collector (in public reputation perhaps the equivalent of drug dealers today). It would be instructive, but sobering, to set our prayers alongside these two.

The paradox of humbling and exaltation is captured in John Wesley's rebuke to an over-confident young preacher whose sermon foundered: 'Sir, if you had entered that pulpit in the manner that you left it, you would have left it in the manner that you entered it.'

Gracious Father,
by the obedience of Jesus
you brought salvation to our wayward world:
draw us into harmony with your will,
that we may find all things restored in him,
our Saviour Jesus Christ.

COLLECT

33

Wednesday 18 June

Psalm 119.105-128
Judges 15.1 – 16.3
Luke 18.15-30

Luke 18.15-30

Jesus calls for 'little children' (infants) to be brought to him for blessing despite the disciples' objections. His reasoning is not that infants possess particular qualities or achievements that make them fit to enter the kingdom, but that lacking such things, they can receive God's love as a free gift of grace – as we all must.

This does not mean that entry into the kingdom is totally unconditional. The rich young man is confident that, through obeying the commandments, he is fit to inherit eternal life. Jesus dispels this illusion by showing his lifelong evasion of the prohibition of covetousness. The instruction to sell his possessions, to give to the poor and follow Jesus reveals that he depends on his wealth: he is not able to let go of it in order to serve God.

Like the bystanders in the story, we in our consumer society should be troubled by the difficulty of the rich entering the kingdom. We are told that God will do whatever human beings cannot. Peter's suggestion that the disciples will be acceptable because they have heeded Jesus' call is not reassuring. We may be left questioning whether and how our attachment to an affluent way of life has made us deaf to the call.

COLLECT

O God, the protector of all who trust in you,
without whom nothing is strong, nothing is holy:
increase and multiply upon us your mercy;
that with you as our ruler and guide
we may so pass through things temporal
that we lose not our hold on things eternal;
grant this, heavenly Father,
for our Lord Jesus Christ's sake,
who is alive and reigns with you,
in the unity of the Holy Spirit,
one God, now and for ever.

Psalms 90, **92**
Judges 16.4-end
Luke 18.31-end

Luke 18.31-end

With Jerusalem drawing ever nearer, Jesus alludes for the third time to his imminent arrest, humiliation, killing and rising. Luke, as always, presents these events as the fulfilment of prophecy and, therefore, part of the divine purpose. However, their meaning remains hidden from the disciples.

This may be for at least two reasons: first, the prospect of Jesus being treated thus was unthinkable for them; and secondly, the events had to take place before they could even begin to understand them. The death of Jesus is profoundly disruptive, both too bad and too good to comprehend and assimilate in normal terms – as Paul describes it, the 'foolishness of God' that is wiser than human wisdom. Only God himself, through the risen Christ, can reveal its saving truth to those who seek.

After this, the healing of the blind beggar is heavy with symbolism. Persistence is rewarded as the man (named Bartimaeus by Mark) cries out for Jesus against the disapproval of those around him. Jesus draws out his request for sight to be restored, and tells him that his faith has saved him. He immediately follows Jesus, his acknowledgement of the 'Son of David' amid the gathering crowds uniting the way of discipleship with the way to the cross.

Gracious Father,
by the obedience of Jesus
you brought salvation to our wayward world:
draw us into harmony with your will,
that we may find all things restored in him,
our Saviour Jesus Christ.

COLLECT

35

Friday 20 June

Psalms **88** (95)
Judges 17
Luke 19.1-10

Luke 19.1-10

The much-loved story of Zacchaeus has an ugly background, for the people are strongly hostile to the fraudulent tax-collector. He may have heard of Jesus as a friend of his class, and he tries to watch unseen by climbing a tree. His efforts to hide are foiled when Jesus looks up and invites himself to his house – a brave and astonishing act.

Jesus' visit provokes the usual complaints from those who consider it unfitting for him to associate with the unworthy; yet he comes not with tolerant indulgence but costly grace. Confronted by this, Zacchaeus is ashamed of his dishonesty and agrees to give to the poor and make restitution on a lavish scale. This is a climactic moment in the Gospel, evoking the ringing assertion that 'the Son of Man came to seek out and to save the lost'.

Sharing the good news of salvation is both breathtakingly powerful and genuinely risky. In coming together, both Jesus and Zacchaeus stand fast against the forces of social and religious condemnation. Today, the story is used as the pattern for a victim awareness programme for offenders. We must look to discern where salvation comes today, and what it costs – remembering that identifying with sinners took Jesus from the house of Zacchaeus to the Place of a Skull.

COLLECT

O God, the protector of all who trust in you,
without whom nothing is strong, nothing is holy:
increase and multiply upon us your mercy;
that with you as our ruler and guide
we may so pass through things temporal
that we lose not our hold on things eternal;
grant this, heavenly Father,
for our Lord Jesus Christ's sake,
who is alive and reigns with you,
in the unity of the Holy Spirit,
one God, now and for ever.

Psalms 96, **97**, 100
Judges 18.1-20, 27-end
Luke 19.11-27

Luke 19.11-27

It is apparent to the reader that Luke here combines two very different plots in one story. Why does he present Jesus telling such a confusing tale? In the parable, the master who leaves money for his servants to trade with becomes identified with a nobleman who goes abroad to claim the crown of his own country, despite the opposition of some of his future subjects. This is modelled closely on the actions of Archelaus, son of Herod the Great, after his father's death.

An explanation is supplied in the opening verse: as Jesus approached Jerusalem, some expected the kingdom of God to come immediately. Instead, Jesus seems to be saying, he will go away in order to return – in his death, resurrection and ascension. The parable ends with the king returning and ordering the slaughter of those who had rebelled: so the crucified Messiah will return to judge and reign.

Meanwhile, the other strand of the parable presses home the lesson that during the master's absence, the servants must be faithful in the task entrusted to them. The disciples are to use the time remaining to complete Jesus' mission to the outcast. Some 2000 years later, we must work out what that requires of us in our world.

Gracious Father,
by the obedience of Jesus
you brought salvation to our wayward world:
draw us into harmony with your will,
that we may find all things restored in him,
our Saviour Jesus Christ.

COLLECT

Monday 23 June

Psalms **98**, 99, 101
I Samuel 1.1-20
Luke 19.28-40

Luke 19.28-40

In one of his hymns, Sidney Cox declares: 'I want to tell you what the Lord has done!' It has a rousing, upbeat tune and reflects the same kind of excitement I imagine the disciples demonstrating as they burst into shouts of praise while walking down the Mount of Olives. They had experienced many amazing things on their travels with Jesus, and now, as they approached Jerusalem, they wanted to make sure everyone knew about it – even those in the crowd who insisted that they should be quiet.

Cox's hymn goes on to say: 'What God has done, he still can do' – and we don't have to look too far to find evidence of the truth of that claim in today's world. The transformation brought about in the lives of individuals and communities when God's love, justice, mercy and peace provide the basis for human relationships is evident in so many situations around the world. The trouble is that we don't talk about them enough, leaving the stage clear for those who argue that faith in God is a dangerous and damaging delusion to make their voices heard loud and clear. If we seriously want to challenge that view, then perhaps those of us who have experienced what God can do need to be a bit more vociferous about it.

COLLECT

Almighty and everlasting God,
by whose Spirit the whole body of the Church
    is governed and sanctified:
hear our prayer which we offer for all your faithful people,
that in their vocation and ministry
they may serve you in holiness and truth
to the glory of your name;
through our Lord and Saviour Jesus Christ,
who is alive and reigns with you,
in the unity of the Holy Spirit,
one God, now and for ever.

Psalms 50, 149
Ecclesiasticus 48.1-10
or Malachi 3.1-6
Luke 3.1-17

The Birth of John the Baptist

Luke 3.1-17

John the Baptist certainly didn't hesitate to make his voice heard – and his uncompromising message not only upset people, it eventually led to his death. Two millennia later, his words hit home with a force that still takes the breath away. Tradition and inheritance are not enough, he declares; nor, it seems, is baptism. All must repent and be baptized for the forgiveness of sins, but repentance must result in practical action. Those who have food and clothing must share with those who have not, and those in positions of authority (tax collectors, soldiers, police, etc.) must change their ways and behave honestly and ethically in their business dealings. This was a really revolutionary idea. The Pharisees would have regarded these jobs as questionable, to say the least, and they would have expected any self-respecting rabbi to tell people to resign from them. Jesus doesn't do that. He tells them that their repentance must affect the way they do their jobs.

In a society so often dominated by attitudes of self-interest, that's a message we must remember. The followers of Jesus, and especially those in positions of influence and power, should be chief among those calling for the needs of the poorest and the most vulnerable in our communities to be addressed fairly and honestly. It's part of our task as people called to 'prepare the way' for the coming of the kingdom of God.

Almighty God,
by whose providence your servant John the Baptist
was wonderfully born,
and sent to prepare the way of your Son our Saviour
by the preaching of repentance:
lead us to repent according to his preaching
and, after his example,
constantly to speak the truth, boldly to rebuke vice,
and patiently to suffer for the truth's sake;
through Jesus Christ your Son our Lord,
who is alive and reigns with you,
in the unity of the Holy Spirit,
one God, now and for ever.

COLLECT

39

Wednesday 25 June

Psalms 110, 111, 112
1 Samuel 2.12-26
Luke 20.1-8

Luke 20.1-8

Jesus is teaching in the temple precincts, and the temple authorities are not happy about it at all. They send a deputation to demand that he tell them what authority he has for his ministry. His response presents them with a dilemma. He asks them where John the Baptist's authority came from, and, backed into a corner, all they can manage is a weak 'We don't know'. Jesus' response is to refuse to answer the question and to leave people to draw their own conclusions on the question of his authority.

We can draw parallels with religious leaders, past and present, who have challenged received wisdom and established authority, and who present us with the dilemma of not knowing how to respond to them – people who both scare and stimulate us with their new and radical ideas of what God is calling the Church to be in this generation. Perhaps the answer lies in examining the 'fruits of repentance' we read about yesterday, and being ready to embrace that which is in harmony with the message of the kingdom, even when it means our own preconceived ideas have got to change.

COLLECT

Almighty and everlasting God,
by whose Spirit the whole body of the Church
    is governed and sanctified:
hear our prayer which we offer for all your faithful people,
that in their vocation and ministry
they may serve you in holiness and truth
to the glory of your name;
through our Lord and Saviour Jesus Christ,
who is alive and reigns with you,
in the unity of the Holy Spirit,
one God, now and for ever.

Luke 20.9-19

There can be no denying Jesus' skill as a storyteller. He was a master of the craft. His stories always contained significant teaching for his listeners and, frequently, as on this occasion, stern rebukes for his opponents. What is worth noting in this story is that, although it is a clear condemnation of the scribes and the chief priests (so clear that even they couldn't miss it!), they were in trouble not for being dilatory but for rebellion against their employer. The servants wanted his property. They wanted to become the master, and were prepared to go to any lengths to get it, even murder. This message was not lost on priests or people.

The temptation is still around, of course, and nowhere more than in the Church. The thirst for power, status and control within the institution often gets in the way of the servant ministry to which the Christian community is called. Sometimes, this is to the extent that it appears as if Christ, the sure foundation, has been rejected in favour of some other cornerstone. Of course, what is true institutionally is equally true individually, which is why this story should make us stop and examine our own aims and objectives a little more regularly than we might.

Almighty God,
send down upon your Church
the riches of your Spirit,
and kindle in all who minister the gospel
your countless gifts of grace;
through Jesus Christ our Lord.

COLLECT

41

Friday 27 June

Psalm 139
1 Samuel 3.1 – 4.1a
Luke 20.20-26

Luke 20.20-26

None too happy at the way the tables had been turned on them, the religious leaders try to trip Jesus up using questions about loyalty. To whom is it owed – God or the emperor? Once again, the plan fails. Jesus' answer, in harmony with Jewish teaching, is that it is owed to both. In things pertaining to the state, obey the state, remembering always, however, that your first duty is to be obedient to God.

On the specific question, Jesus' response was enough to avoid charges of treason, but on the wider canvas, the loyalty question remains a live one for people of faith. What is the Christian to do when matters of faith and law collide? When the state seeks to introduce policies that blatantly contradict the Gospel imperative to love God and to love our neighbours as ourselves? Heroes of the faith like Dietrich Bonhoeffer and Desmond Tutu show clearly what the answer should be. God promises to provide the courage, grace and strength to enable us to follow their example and give it.

COLLECT

Almighty and everlasting God,
by whose Spirit the whole body of the Church
    is governed and sanctified:
hear our prayer which we offer for all your faithful people,
that in their vocation and ministry
they may serve you in holiness and truth
to the glory of your name;
through our Lord and Saviour Jesus Christ,
who is alive and reigns with you,
in the unity of the Holy Spirit,
one God, now and for ever.

Psalms 120, **121**, 122
1 Samuel 4.1b-end
Luke 20.27-40

Luke 20.27-40

Today's reading brings us to the climax of the disputes raised with Jesus about his teaching. The issue on this occasion is the question of resurrection and its implications for women, who, having been widowed, remarry in line with the law of Moses. Behind the question lies the implication that resurrection must be a false doctrine, but theargument is based on a false premise, and one that is still around today.

People frequently think of resurrection life as being governed by the same norms, conditions and conventions as the here and now. It is not. Resurrection life is a completely transformed state of existence, one in which we are 'changed from glory into glory'. Things that serve as partial, but important, indicators in the here and now of what that life will be like, such as marriage and having children, will become irrelevant as human relationships are raised to a new level and as the fundamental relationship of being a child of God is fully realized. Coming to Christ establishes that relationship, and living the Christian life witnesses to the world that resurrection life is both possible and under way. To that end, may we, who share Christ's body, truly live his risen life.

Almighty God,
send down upon your Church
the riches of your Spirit,
and kindle in all who minister the gospel
your countless gifts of grace;
through Jesus Christ our Lord.

COLLECT

43

Psalms 123, 124, 125, **126**
1 Samuel 5
Luke 20.41 – 21.4

Luke 20.41 – 21.4

There were very few ways for a widow to earn a living in first-century Judea. Life was tough, and poverty and widowhood usually went hand in hand, hence the reason for the marriage law referred to in verse 27. The woman in this story was clearly very poor indeed, as her gift of two small copper coins was just about the minimum permitted – yet, according to Jesus, she gave more than anyone else. She gave everything and, in doing so, demonstrated her faith and trust in God. Here, Luke is making clear that, as Howard Marshall puts it, 'what matters is not the amount that one gives but the amount that one keeps for oneself'. That provides a way of distinguishing between true and false piety, which is why this story is set alongside Jesus' criticism of the scribes.

The picture painted of the scribes is of a group of people who use their position for their own ends and who cloak their avarice and ambition under a veil of religiosity. Their greed is so great that they will even 'devour widows' houses'. Their behaviour earned them the condemnation of Christ, as will the behaviour of all who use positions of trust to serve themselves rather than others.

COLLECT

Merciful God,
you have prepared for those who love you
such good things as pass our understanding:
pour into our hearts such love toward you
that we, loving you in all things and above all things,
may obtain your promises,
which exceed all that we can desire;
through Jesus Christ your Son our Lord,
who is alive and reigns with you,
in the unity of the Holy Spirit,
one God, now and for ever.

44

Psalms **132**, 133
1 Samuel 6.1-16
Luke 21.5-19

Luke 21.5-19

Predictions that the end of the world is imminent are not a new phenomenon; they have surfaced frequently through the ages, especially at moments of major change in society such as the one in which Luke was living. By the time he wrote his Gospel, Christians had been subjected to persecution, torture and martyrdom, Jerusalem had fallen, the temple had been destroyed and natural disasters had taken place in the region. Understandably, many thought that the end was nigh and tried to use these signs to calculate when it would be. Jesus' teaching is that his followers should not be preoccupied with speculation like this, nor should they panic or be afraid in the face of millenarian propaganda. Patience, discernment and endurance are to be the hallmarks of believers as they try to live the life of Christian discipleship – then and now.

Christians today should not be panicked by what they see and hear around them into becoming preoccupied with the end of the world. Rather, by living as a community of people who know what our ultimate destiny is to be, we are to lay before the world the message of hope, reconciliation and new life we have encountered in Christ.

Creator God,
you made us all in your image:
may we discern you in all that we see,
and serve you in all that we do;
through Jesus Christ our Lord.

COLLECT

Wednesday 2 July

Luke 21.20-28

Joy Webb and the Joystrings were one of the first 'worship bands' in the United Kingdom. This Salvation Army group became so popular that they even made it into the charts alongside the Beatles and the Rolling Stones in the 1960s, which is something hard to imagine any worship band achieving today! One of the Joystrings' songs summed up the message of Luke in this section of the Gospel.

The song contained the couplet, 'in the pain, in the doubt, in the loneliness, in the struggle of right against wrong, somewhere amidst the confusion, there will be hope, there will be love, there will be God', and, as Luke continues his apocalyptic theme, this is exactly his message. He paints an even more graphic picture than before, in which there is even greater confusion and deeper despair in the face of the utter destruction of all that is. Yet, at the point at which the final curtain appears to be falling on the whole of creation, the Son of Man appears 'with power and great glory'. This is the time to look up, not down, he says, for amid all the chaos and destruction, God will be found. That will be true at the end of all things, but it is equally true now in those moments when we feel perplexed, confused and afraid. If we look up, we'll discover we're not alone.

COLLECT

Merciful God,
you have prepared for those who love you
such good things as pass our understanding:
pour into our hearts such love toward you
that we, loving you in all things and above all things,
may obtain your promises,
which exceed all that we can desire;
through Jesus Christ your Son our Lord,
who is alive and reigns with you,
in the unity of the Holy Spirit,
one God, now and for ever.

Psalms 92, 146
2 Samuel 15.17-21 *or*
Ecclesiasticus 2
John 11.1-16

Thomas the Apostle

John 11.1-16

The Gospel reading for the Eucharist today is the one that most people associate with Thomas: it records his doubts when he is told of the resurrection. The reference to him at the end of this story is much less well known, understandably so, for here the focus is on Martha, Mary and Lazarus. To understand Thomas' words, they need to be seen in the context of the events referred to in verse 7. John 10 records the failed attempt to do away with Jesus, after which he escapes across the Jordan. Now, in deciding to go to Lazarus, he was taking himself back into the very centre of the danger zone, Bethany being less than two miles from Jerusalem. Thomas says what the others are almost certainly thinking and acknowledges that going would be an almost suicidal act. Even so, he sets his face against desertion and takes the lead in following Jesus back to Jerusalem.

It is not the kind of resolute action we generally associate with Thomas, but it is a clear demonstration of what it takes to be a saint – being prepared to face up to the very real demands of discipleship, whatever the cost.

Almighty and eternal God,
who, for the firmer foundation of our faith,
allowed your holy apostle Thomas
to doubt the resurrection of your Son
till word and sight convinced him:
grant to us, who have not seen, that we also may believe
and so confess Christ as our Lord and our God;
who is alive and reigns with you,
in the unity of the Holy Spirit,
one God, now and for ever.

COLLECT

Friday 4 July

Psalms 142, **144**
1 Samuel 9.1-14
Luke 22.1-13

Luke 22.1-13

When it comes to the considering the cost of discipleship, the yardstick has to be the total commitment and trust we see as the final days of the life of Jesus unfold. The first stages begin here. The Jewish leaders are looking for a way to have done with Jesus without causing a riot among the Passover pilgrims; Judas, having decided to betray him, provides them with an opportunity to arrest him with very few people around. In the meantime, Jesus makes his own plans to celebrate the Passover with his followers, including Judas, in the city itself.

So many questions bubble up when considering all of this. Why did Judas do what he did? Greed? Frustration? Political ambition? And why did Jesus set his face so resolutely towards Jerusalem, knowing that whatever lay ahead it would not be pleasant? The answers all have to do with obedience. Whatever was going on in Judas' head, he chose to turn away from God's will, and whatever huge turmoil there was in Jesus' mind, he chose to accept and follow it. We know the dilemma only too well, and are all too well aware of our own moments of betrayal. I sometimes wonder if that is why there is no vilification of Judas by any of the evangelists. They, too, knew what it was to fail the Lord.

COLLECT

Merciful God,
you have prepared for those who love you
such good things as pass our understanding:
pour into our hearts such love toward you
that we, loving you in all things and above all things,
may obtain your promises,
which exceed all that we can desire;
through Jesus Christ your Son our Lord,
who is alive and reigns with you,
in the unity of the Holy Spirit,
one God, now and for ever.

Luke 22.14-23

It is quite impossible to explore the mysteries of the Last Supper in a few short words. Theologians have discussed it at length, and textual scholars have attempted to address the difficulties raised by the variants in the narratives by trying to piece together the chronology of the events described. What we can do is reflect briefly on what might be meant by the words, 'Do this in remembrance of me.'

The biblical category of memory (*anamnesis*) is remembrance that makes the thing remembered actually present. This an important aspect of eucharistic remembrance – for, whatever else it is about, the starting point is that Jesus' final bequest at the Last Supper is of himself and of his enduring presence with those who belong to him. We may not be able to comprehend *how* his abiding presence is made real through the signs and symbols of bread and wine; what matters is that it *is*, and, as a result, every celebration becomes a moment of divine communion in which his presence becomes very real to us as we are drawn deeper into him.

Creator God,
you made us all in your image:
may we discern you in all that we see,
and serve you in all that we do;
through Jesus Christ our Lord.

COLLECT

Monday 7 July

Luke 22.24-30

Being with Jesus was intoxicating. It wasn't just all the talk of the kingdom, but also seeing its reality before their very eyes – people restored physically, mentally and socially. There was the heady arrival in Jerusalem, acclaiming his kingship. There was the intimacy of the Passover, a growing sense perhaps of something about to happen. And in this intoxicating mix, having heard that one of them would betray Jesus, the disciples wonder too which of them would be the greatest.

Having the rug pulled out from under your feet, coming down to earth with a bump – whichever image you prefer, the outcome is still the same: a sudden, ungainly and painful grounding. Jesus does not allow such thoughts to develop. Greatness in his kingdom means that those at table with him are to be like those who serve, like the youngest, the least important.

And yet ... it's a bit of a roller-coaster – no sooner down than up again. They will sit at table with him in his kingdom; not just that but on thrones too. What kind of kingdom is this? Perhaps our biggest mistake would be to get carried away with thinking we know.

COLLECT

Lord of all power and might,
the author and giver of all good things:
graft in our hearts the love of your name,
increase in us true religion,
nourish us with all goodness,
and of your great mercy keep us in the same;
through Jesus Christ your Son our Lord,
who is alive and reigns with you,
in the unity of the Holy Spirit,
one God, now and for ever.

Psalms **5**, 6 (8)
1 Samuel 10.17-end
Luke 22.31-38

Luke 22.31-38

In C. S. Lewis' *Prince Caspian*, Aslan greets the sceptical Trumpkin by tossing him high into the air and catching him in velvety paws. It's a terrifying experience for the dwarf, but for those already 'in the know', confidence in Aslan dispels any fear for their friend. A similar image comes to mind here, only it's far less comforting. We are reminded of Job, whom Satan was permitted to test. If he is allowed to sift the disciples like wheat being tossed into the air to remove the chaff, what will remain?

Jesus knows the answer to that question. He knows, too, that a time of conflict lies ahead. He knows that Simon Peter has to face his own failures before he can be the kind of disciple he wants himself to be. Most important of all, he knows Peter's true worth.

The disciples were not party to Jesus' testing by Satan, early in Luke's narrative, but Luke makes it clear that by following Jesus, we are in this conflict too. Here, we see Satan the accuser, one who seeks to put us in situations that will expose our weaknesses. The startling thing, though, is not the strength of our faith in Jesus, but – knowing us as he does – of his in us.

Generous God,
you give us gifts and make them grow:
though our faith is small as mustard seed,
make it grow to your glory
and the flourishing of your kingdom;
through Jesus Christ our Lord.

COLLECT

Wednesday 9 July

Luke 22.39-46

Approaching the Chapel of Christ in Gethsemane in Coventry Cathedral, one comes face to face with the angel, seen through a crown of thorns. This figure, bearing a cup and bathed in gold, conveying warmth and strength, fills the back wall of the chapel. It captures the attention of those standing before it. We might be forgiven for failing to notice the sleeping disciples, portrayed in relief on the wall to the right. The artist has captured them in their total exhaustion, unable to be with Jesus in the way he has asked. Not that long ago, they were wondering who would be the greatest in the kingdom. Now the scene is much darker: totally overcome by grief at what is developing, they are oblivious to anything around them.

We live with an inescapable awareness of human suffering; no one is untouched by it. However much we know in our heads that following Jesus means staying with him in suffering, we still in our heart wish for the 'magic wand' solution, an instant putting right of all that is wrong. For us, as for Jesus, that is not for now. The presence of the angel does not bring about an end to the agony, but the strength to stay with it and see it through to its conclusion.

COLLECT

Lord of all power and might,
the author and giver of all good things:
graft in our hearts the love of your name,
increase in us true religion,
nourish us with all goodness,
and of your great mercy keep us in the same;
through Jesus Christ your Son our Lord,
who is alive and reigns with you,
in the unity of the Holy Spirit,
one God, now and for ever.

Psalms 14, **15**, 16
1 Samuel 12
Luke 22.47-62

Luke 22.47-62

Suddenly the spotlights are on. A scene of darkness and isolation, stillness and intimacy, gives way to one of activity and crowds. The traitorous kiss is given, a sword is drawn, blood is shed. It is dramatic, theatrical – and flawed. It is the working-out of a resolution to bring an end to that which is good and life-giving. It is a display of power, by those who cannot see the true extent of the territory over which the battle is being fought.

And yet – one wonders who is turning the spotlight upon whom. Jesus knows what Judas is about, and knows the fear and weakness that lie behind the night-time arrest. His words highlight the disproportion between what is done and the manner of doing it.

Similarly, for Peter in the courtyard, it is evident that, though it may be Satan's desire to uncover our weaknesses, it is in the clear light of Jesus' gaze that we see them. What Satan does is expose us to God. God's response is not to reject, but to offer restoration.

Generous God,
you give us gifts and make them grow:
though our faith is small as mustard seed,
make it grow to your glory
and the flourishing of your kingdom;
through Jesus Christ our Lord.

COLLECT

53

Friday 11 July

Luke 22.63-end

A fundamental procedure of the courtroom is that all defendants, no matter what else they say, must confirm their identity. It is a basic matter of verification, the matching of a flesh-and-blood person to a name on the paperwork. Here, however, there is no paperwork, and for the Council, it is the question of identity that is itself on trial. No paperwork perhaps, but centuries of experience of God. No paperwork, but writings that testify to the identity of the nation called into relationship with him, and to the character of the God who calls.

What is the nature of the relationship between the Almighty and this Galilean who stands before them? Is he merely that – a Galilean carpenter, Jesus of Nazareth, of no special religious significance? Or is it possible that he is what others claim: the one whom God has appointed to bring salvation to his people? Names and titles from the writings are flung to and fro in the brief exchange of words – Messiah, Son of Man, Son of God. If these apply to Jesus, as he seems to suggest, then the guardians of the religious identity of the people have got it seriously wrong.

COLLECT

Lord of all power and might,
the author and giver of all good things:
graft in our hearts the love of your name,
increase in us true religion,
nourish us with all goodness,
and of your great mercy keep us in the same;
through Jesus Christ your Son our Lord,
who is alive and reigns with you,
in the unity of the Holy Spirit,
one God, now and for ever.

Psalms 20, 21, **23**
1 Samuel 13.19 – 14.15
Luke 23.1-12

Luke 23.1-12

Luke gives no hint of Pilate having any curiosity about Jesus; he was more concerned with the crowd. Herod, however, was agog and – most probably – fearful. Who was this? The dead John the Baptist? Elijah? Rumours had been rife for some time, feeding his troubled conscience. Now face to face, Jesus' silence did nothing to bring him peace of mind.

Friendships flourish on common ground, in the discovery of some sense of inhabiting the same world. Whether or not Jesus presented a real threat to either of these two men was hardly relevant; his accusers made sure that they tailored their accusations to hit home hardest. To Pilate, the foreigner, a cog in the great Roman machine, they insist that he was subversive. To Herod, the Jewish puppet king, it seems that the claims of kingship were emphasized.

They may have thought themselves to be worlds apart, but, in the process of sending Jesus back and forth, Pilate and Herod came to see that they looked out upon the same landscape. Their shared world was one in which religion and power came together in a heady and often violent mix. They discovered a common mind in the necessity of maintaining the status quo.

Generous God,
you give us gifts and make them grow:
though our faith is small as mustard seed,
make it grow to your glory
and the flourishing of your kingdom;
through Jesus Christ our Lord.

COLLECT

Monday 14 July

Luke 23.13-25

There is a stage in childhood in which the conviction is evident that if you shout loud enough, you get your own way. In adulthood, this can become: 'If I say it loud enough *and* long enough, not only will I get my own way, but also others will come to believe that what I am saying is true.' It is a trait evident in some branches of the media.

Luke tells us three times that Pilate does not find Jesus guilty of the charges brought against him. Three times this verdict is met with ever louder demands for his death. What does Pilate do? He gives in. Power lies with those who shout the loudest.

There are times in life when there is simply nothing good to be said. Events that affect us, and the behaviour of those around us are all contrary to that which is good. We feel helpless, starved of the hope of anything good. As Christians, perhaps we burden ourselves with the feeling that we *ought* to be able to find something positive in such a situation, that there must be some chink of light.

Pilate's capitulation extinguishes any hope of a way out for Jesus. No angel hovers to whisper that actually everything will be all right. Only death lies ahead.

COLLECT

Almighty Lord and everlasting God,
we beseech you to direct, sanctify and govern
    both our hearts and bodies
in the ways of your laws
    and the works of your commandments;
that through your most mighty protection, both here and ever,
we may be preserved in body and soul;
through our Lord and Saviour Jesus Christ,
who is alive and reigns with you,
in the unity of the Holy Spirit,
one God, now and for ever.

Psalms 32, **36**
1 Samuel 15.1-23
Luke 23.26-43

Luke 23.26-43

In the Anglo-Saxon poem, *The Dream of the Rood*, Jesus embraces the cross as a warrior king engaging in mortal combat. It was considered degrading for an Anglo-Saxon king to display weakness and suffer humiliation in battle. So, while Jesus is 'strong and unflinching', the poet makes the cross itself experience the torment of crucifixion. Is this unrealistic? Not for Luke, who leaves us in no doubt, even here at this point of utter human vulnerability, of the kingship of Jesus.

Here we have a mirror image of the triumphal entry into Jerusalem: not arriving, acclaimed as king, but leaving, accompanied by tears. Not a mounted king, but a beaten man going to a criminal's death, too weak to bear the physical weight demanded of him. All aspirations of kingship are surely utterly shattered.

And yet ... we hear echoes of the Song of Songs, the bride addressing the 'daughters of Jerusalem', summoning them to come out and see King Solomon, crowned, passing by. We hear him speak, evoking the prophet Hosea's words of judgement from God on his idolatrous people. With 'king' and 'Messiah', the leaders think they mock, but there is truth in the plea of the second criminal: the kingdom is near. In the face of cruelty and shattered hopes, we are not to lose sight of the sovereignty of God.

Lord God,
your Son left the riches of heaven
and became poor for our sake:
when we prosper save us from pride,
when we are needy save us from despair,
that we may trust in you alone;
through Jesus Christ our Lord.

COLLECT

Wednesday 16 July

Luke 23.44-56a

Some things are so big and so deep that they cannot easily be spoken of. They need to be expressed in other ways to allow the audience space to enter into the experience. This might be in the feelings evoked by music, or in the space to reflect offered by the visual arts. Or it might, as here, be in the weaving of a narrative.

Luke could have chosen to describe a routine crucifixion, then gone on to what happened next; or he could have stated his theology of atonement. Neither would have been adequate. Instead, he tells his story in such a way that we see and hear more than if we had been physically there, and we sense the momentous nature of what is taking place. In the darkening of the sun, the self-surrendering cry of Jesus, and, supremely, in the tearing of the temple curtain, we too are left momentarily breathless, stunned by the revelation that somehow, in this whole moment, that which divided us from God has gone – for ever.

Something of this is perceived by the centurion; the remorseful crowd sees only the death. Joseph sees what needs to be done, and gets on with it. Luke leaves us with the women, waiting.

COLLECT

Almighty Lord and everlasting God,
we beseech you to direct, sanctify and govern
    both our hearts and bodies
in the ways of your laws
    and the works of your commandments;
that through your most mighty protection, both here and ever,
we may be preserved in body and soul;
through our Lord and Saviour Jesus Christ,
who is alive and reigns with you,
in the unity of the Holy Spirit,
one God, now and for ever.

Psalm **37***
1 Samuel 17.1-30
Luke 23.56b – 24.12

Luke 23.56b – 24.12

Did Peter go to the tomb thinking only to put a stop to this 'idle tale', dismissive as he and the other apostles were of the heavenly testimony entrusted to the women? Had he forgotten his own previous experience: Jesus transfigured, his glorious appearance with Moses and Elijah, and the struggle to know how to respond?

The telling of the story was not itself enough for the apostles to believe that Jesus was alive. Something more was needed. What made the difference for Peter was seeing – seeing that something was missing, and then being amazed. What he encountered at the tomb displaced what he thought he knew. This was not in itself belief, but it made space for something new to grow. We are not shown the moment of resurrection, only its effects. None of those who had known Jesus are reassured by his presence straight away. First comes the discovery of the empty space, perplexity and wonder.

Lord God,
your Son left the riches of heaven
and became poor for our sake:
when we prosper save us from pride,
when we are needy save us from despair,
that we may trust in you alone;
through Jesus Christ our Lord.

COLLECT

59

Friday 18 July

Psalm **31**
I Samuel 17.31-54
Luke 24.13-35

Luke 24.13-35

They must have been talking among themselves all day long. It was perhaps a relief to have someone new to tell it all to – a stranger, who was, in effect, a 'blank sheet'. What did they make of the response they got? Jesus is not a *kind* teacher; he does not spare these two, but confronts them with the folly of their failure to understand. Luke does not tell us where they were when he first fell in beside them, but it seems that he gave them a good few miles of explanations.

If they had been with Jesus all that time, and saw yet did not comprehend, what chance do we have? The talking goes on. *The Da Vinci Code* was by no means the first book to seek to bring Jesus within parameters that we can understand; we can be sure it will not be the last. And Luke's view? – listen to the risen Jesus; let him be our interpreter.

So, what did they perceive when guest became host and those hands took and broke the bread? All that they knew of a life shared and given away; all that they had yet to discover of a life endlessly giving and nourishing. No wonder they went straight back to tell the others.

COLLECT

Almighty Lord and everlasting God,
we beseech you to direct, sanctify and govern
    both our hearts and bodies
in the ways of your laws
    and the works of your commandments;
that through your most mighty protection, both here and ever,
we may be preserved in body and soul;
through our Lord and Saviour Jesus Christ,
who is alive and reigns with you,
in the unity of the Holy Spirit,
one God, now and for ever.

Psalms 41, **42**, 43
1 Samuel 17.55-18.16
Luke 24.36-end

Saturday 19 July

Luke 24.36-end

Here we are, reading the end – for now – of Luke's story. Perhaps we feel relief: here's a happy ending, a quick tying-up of loose ends. It might almost be true to say they all lived happily ever after. It's like a cosy jumper and a cup of cocoa at the end of a busy day ...

It isn't, though, is it? Luke tells of fear and doubt. How did it feel to be there – to touch, to see and to hear Jesus once more? Did they feel foolish, as if they ought to have known what was going on all along? Is that Jesus' meaning? Or is he opening their minds to the fact that the ways of God are nearly always about things being bigger, better and more wonderful than we can ever think for ourselves?

Like the disciples, we have to meet Jesus with an open mind. Reading in this way can mean being profoundly disturbed – being open to his presence, accepting the consequences of suffering, resurrection, repentance, forgiveness. It's such a lot to take in that retreat to the cosy jumper has quite an appeal. But the promise of Jesus holds so much more: a complete clothing, with power from on high. And so (as T. S. Eliot says in *Little Gidding*), the end is where we start from.

Lord God,
your Son left the riches of heaven
and became poor for our sake:
when we prosper save us from pride,
when we are needy save us from despair,
that we may trust in you alone;
through Jesus Christ our Lord.

COLLECT

Monday 21 July

Psalm **44**
1 Samuel 19.1-18
Acts 1.1-14

Acts 1.1-14

Although this book is called 'Acts of the Apostles', I reckon 'Gospel of the Holy Spirit' might be a better name. This sequel to Luke's Gospel is going to be a Spirit-filled story of a Spirit-led movement of change.

Both books are addressed to someone called Theophilus. We're not sure who this is – perhaps a Roman official investigating the Christian movement – but his name means 'beloved of God'. In which case, let us imagine it is us! God's beloved, invited to participate in his story.

We start at the Ascension. The bewildered disciples stare into the sky, wondering where Jesus has gone. This is a hinge event for Luke. His Gospel ends, and this book begins, with this strange story of arrival and departure. Jesus' mission is complete. He departs from the earth and takes humanity into heaven. The mission of his Church begins. The apostles await the arrival of the Spirit, which is the new presence of Jesus no longer constrained by space and time. It is about absence and presence. Jesus is absent to them in the flesh, but will soon be present to them in a new and dynamic way. The disciples are about to be woken with a start. They think it is all over. It is only just beginning.

COLLECT

Almighty God,
who sent your Holy Spirit
to be the life and light of your Church:
open our hearts to the riches of your grace,
that we may bring forth the fruit of the Spirit
in love and joy and peace;
through Jesus Christ your Son our Lord,
who is alive and reigns with you,
in the unity of the Holy Spirit,
one God, now and for ever.

Psalms 30, 32, 150
I Samuel 16.14-23
Luke 8.1-3

Tuesday 22 July

Mary Magdalene

Luke 8.1-3

To honour Mary Magdalene, we come out of the Acts of the Apostles and into the Gospel of Luke. But it is still an apostle of Jesus that we are remembering: not one of the Twelve, but a woman esteemed by the Church for her faithfulness to Jesus and her proclamation of the gospel.

Jesus' attitude to women is not typical of his time. He accords them great respect. He welcomes them as equals. They are part of the band of disciples who follow him. We also learn here that they are among the main financial supporters of his mission.

There is something else that these women have in common. They have all been healed by Jesus. They follow him out of thankfulness, and they give with joy. This is always the pattern of Christian ministry: we give from the overflow of what we have received.

We can also note that when the going gets really tough, it tends to be the women who stick with Jesus. Hence, it is Mary Magdalene, lingering at the tomb, who is the first witness to the resurrection and gives to the world the first proclamation of Easter joy: 'I have seen the Lord!' (John 20.18).

Almighty God,
whose Son restored Mary Magdalene
to health of mind and body
and called her to be a witness to his resurrection:
forgive our sins and heal us by your grace,
that we may serve you in the power of his risen life;
who is alive and reigns with you,
in the unity of the Holy Spirit,
one God, now and for ever.

COLLECT

63

Wednesday 23 July

Acts 2.1-21

Now we get to the astonishing story of Pentecost itself. The Church is born from the wind and fire of the Spirit.

The wind represents God's power, but is also a reference to God's breath: God's still small voice that spoke to Elijah in his need, and the very breath that brought life to Adam and Eve in the first place. The fire of the Spirit that illuminates but does not consume reminds us of the burning bush out of which God spoke to Moses, and the burning fiery furnace that could not overwhelm the faith of Shadrach, Meshach and Abednego when they were asked to worship a statue made from human hands. The remarkable ability of the disciples to speak in different languages reverses the confusion that was brought into the world at Babel, when human vanity and greed created warring faction from harmonious diversity. Joel's prophecy that one day all God's people will receive God's spirit is dramatically fulfilled.

All these Old Testament stories and prophecies are consummated as the disciples – thought to be drunk with wine – pour onto the streets of Jerusalem telling of God's love in Christ, drunk on the intoxicating joy of the Spirit. A new age begins, where everyone who calls on the name of the Lord will be saved. This spirit is available to everyone.

COLLECT

Almighty God,
who sent your Holy Spirit
to be the life and light of your Church:
open our hearts to the riches of your grace,
that we may bring forth the fruit of the Spirit
in love and joy and peace;
through Jesus Christ your Son our Lord,
who is alive and reigns with you,
in the unity of the Holy Spirit,
one God, now and for ever.

Psalms 56, **57** (63*)
I Samuel 21.1 – 22.5
Acts 2.22-36

Thursday 24 July

Acts 2.22-36

Standing in the street at just after nine in the morning, surrounded by people from many nations who have gathered in Jerusalem for the feast, Peter preaches the first sermon in Christian history. And, although countless millions of sermons have been preached since, has any Christian preacher ever had anything else worth saying? For the scandalous heart of the Christian gospel is not some human philosophy, no matter how edifying or wise, but a blunt and basic proclamation that this Jesus who was crucified has been raised to life. What is offered? What is said? Nothing other than that this motley band of Palestinian fishermen and assorted odd-bods are witnesses to God's breaking into history. Furthermore, this has been God's plan from the beginning. All the Jewish Scriptures actually point to this decisive event where God makes peace with the world through the shed blood of Christ and creates a new humanity. The gift of the Spirit is the sign that this rescue mission is complete, and that a new age of a new availability to God has commenced.

Nothing will ever be the same again. Let all Israel know – and soon, as we shall see, the entire world – this Jesus whom you crucified; God has made him both Lord and Messiah.

Gracious Father,
revive your Church in our day,
and make her holy, strong and faithful,
for your glory's sake
in Jesus Christ our Lord.

COLLECT

65

Friday 25 July

James the Apostle

Psalms 7, 29, 117
2 Kings 1.9-15
Luke 9.46-56

Luke 9.46-56

Today, we turn again to Luke's Gospel to consider the great apostle James. But the lectionary doesn't let us dwell on James' undoubted strengths. Rather, we read about how much he got it wrong: wanting a place at Jesus' right hand, arguing over who was greatest, and then suggesting that an entire village of Samaritans should be ethnically cleansed! How easy it is to get it wrong. It is possible to be one of the chosen Twelve and still unerringly miss the point. Indeed, the Twelve consistently display an uncanny knack of picking up the wrong end of almost every stick.

So, goodness and rightness cannot be measured by the titles we amass: not even the title 'apostle'. In Luke's Gospel, it is usually the little people on the edge of the story, the ones who are most in need, who get it right – not by their goodness, but by their thankfulness, and by their acknowledgement of their need. In the end, it is this receiving of grace that best equips us for ministry in God's Church.

COLLECT

Merciful God,
whose holy apostle Saint James,
leaving his father and all that he had,
was obedient to the calling of your Son Jesus Christ
and followed him even to death:
help us, forsaking the false attractions of the world,
to be ready at all times to answer your call without delay;
through Jesus Christ your Son our Lord,
who is alive and reigns with you,
in the unity of the Holy Spirit,
one God, now and for ever.

Psalm **68**
1 Samuel 23
Acts 3.1-10

Acts 3.1-10

The reason it is called the Acts of the Apostles, and not the Gospel of the Holy Spirit, is made evident in this passage: the mighty acts that Jesus did as signs of God's presence are now performed by his followers. This is the second great theme of this book.

Peter and John see the paralysed man. They don't have any money for him, but they do not pass him by. They have learned at last to give from what they have received. They offer what they do possess – the ministry of Jesus. In the name of Jesus of Nazareth (note that they don't even use a technical, theological word like 'Christ': it is just Jesus from Nazareth, the man they have followed, whom God has raised), they bid the man stand up and walk.

As God has raised Jesus, so this man can be raised. They do not do this in their own power, but in the power of the Spirit. They do not do it in their own name, but in the name of Jesus. They do not do it to point to themselves, but to God. The birth of the Church is seen in this story just as much as in the story of Pentecost. In the power of the Spirit, the ministry of Jesus continues through his Church.

Almighty God,
who sent your Holy Spirit
to be the life and light of your Church:
open our hearts to the riches of your grace,
that we may bring forth the fruit of the Spirit
in love and joy and peace;
through Jesus Christ your Son our Lord,
who is alive and reigns with you,
in the unity of the Holy Spirit,
one God, now and for ever.

COLLECT

67

Monday 28 July

Psalm 71
I Samuel 24
Acts 3.11-end

Acts 3.11-end

The Church's second sermon builds on the themes of the first. This miracle is done not by our power, says Peter, but by the one whom you Israelites rejected and killed. We are his witnesses, and what you see is his work, and his alone, and is fulfilment of what God foretold through the prophets.

For the first Jewish listeners to this gospel, the fact that the Messiah suffered and died is a huge stumbling block. As far as they were concerned, the crucifixion was proof that Jesus *couldn't* be the Messiah. Here, then, is a theme of the New Testament: that the passion of Christ is foretold in the prophets (v.18); that this is the true meaning of Scripture.

Peter tells his hearers what to do. He calls them to repent, not as a precondition for receiving what God has done in Christ, but as the only possible response. We got it wrong. We misunderstood the purposes of God. We ended up killing the one whom God sent to save us. But God's love cannot be defeated. It goes on. God has raised Jesus to life. He can raise us. And so, the simple and persistent announcement of what has happened in Christ and of the gift and power of the Spirit becomes the preaching of the Church.

COLLECT

Let your merciful ears, O Lord,
be open to the prayers of your humble servants;
and that they may obtain their petitions
make them to ask such things as shall please you;
through Jesus Christ your Son our Lord,
who is alive and reigns with you,
in the unity of the Holy Spirit,
one God, now and for ever.

Psalm **73**
1 Samuel 26
Acts 4.1-12

Acts 4.1-12

The Church is growing. Another 5000 people have come to believe in Jesus. Having been arrested for teaching about the resurrection, Peter and John are brought before the elders and scribes and are quizzed about the healing of the paralysed man. By what power have they done this? Again, Peter recounts the basic message of the Christian faith. It is not an explanation, but a proclamation. Peter can't necessarily say how it is done, nor even why, but he does know that it is done in the name of Jesus, the one whom they rejected. God has raised him up, and there is salvation in his name.

Luke tells us that Peter speaks in the power of the Spirit (v.8). This is significant. The Spirit is being manifest in different ways: now guiding and strengthening. Jesus had warned his disciples that they would be handed over to councils and dragged before kings. He said to them: 'When they hand you over, do not worry about how you are to speak or what you are to say; for what you are to say will be given to you at that time; for it is not you who speak, but the Spirit of your Father speaking through you' (Matthew 10.19-20).

Lord of heaven and earth,
as Jesus taught his disciples to be persistent in prayer,
give us patience and courage never to lose hope,
but always to bring our prayers before you;
through Jesus Christ our Lord.

COLLECT

69

Wednesday 30 July

Psalm **77**
1 Samuel 28.3-end
Acts 4.13-31

Acts 4.13-31

Faced with the evidence of a lame man walking, what can the scribes do except try to keep a lid on the whole thing? They ask Peter and John to stop speaking in the name of Jesus. But they will do nothing of the sort. Their response is wonderful. They avoid getting into the rights and wrongs of how, or how not, God might be at work in Jesus and who has the authority to judge the matter: 'We cannot keep from speaking about what we have seen and heard' is their straightforward reply.

This is the nub of the evangelistic preaching of the Church – we share what we have experienced and received. The whole preaching of the gospel and, indeed, the whole theology of the Church flow from the experience of what God does in Jesus and continues to do through the Spirit. All our teaching and preaching is the reflection upon this experience, as the Spirit leads us deeper into this truth and as the different questions and obstacles that different cultures pose draw forth fresh insights into this basic proclamation of God's presence among us in Jesus. And so the disciples prayed for boldness to speak God's word. We must do the same today.

COLLECT

Let your merciful ears, O Lord,
be open to the prayers of your humble servants;
and that they may obtain their petitions
make them to ask such things as shall please you;
through Jesus Christ your Son our Lord,
who is alive and reigns with you,
in the unity of the Holy Spirit,
one God, now and for ever.

Psalm **78.1-39***
I Samuel 31
Acts 4.32 – 5.11

Acts 4.32 – 5.11

Today's reading offers two extreme images of what it means to follow Christ. On the one hand, we see the generosity and care that the first Christians show to each other: goods and money are held in common and distributed according to need. This is a beautiful image of the reordering of creation by the infant Church. On the other, we learn of the terrible consequences of holding things back from God. This is a terrible image of the consequence of wilful deceit.

But it is worth noting that it is not the Church that punishes Ananias and Sapphira. All Peter does is point out their failure. But, having reneged on the deal, it is God they have abandoned.

Luke intends us to read this as God's punishment. It is not that God has stopped being loving or forgiving, but we are brought face to face with the reality of consequences. Just as we are free to accept the mercy of God, we are also free to reject it. It is the concealing of the crime, the keeping of things for oneself, the lie, that does the damage. God is faithful to his covenant. We are not, and to place ourselves outside God's covenant of love is death.

Lord of heaven and earth,
as Jesus taught his disciples to be persistent in prayer,
give us patience and courage never to lose hope,
but always to bring our prayers before you;
through Jesus Christ our Lord.

COLLECT

71

Friday 1 August

Psalm **55**
2 Samuel 1
Acts 5.12-26

Acts 5.12-26

Tucked away inside today's reading is one of the most astonishing examples of transformation in the whole Bible. More believers are added to the Church, and now the reputation of the apostles is so great that people even bring their sick out onto the pavement in the hope that Peter's shadow might fall on them as he passes by. Can this be the same person we read about in the Gospels? The same Peter who promised so much, but who always ended up getting it wrong? The same Peter who three times denied he even knew Jesus?

He has received the Holy Spirit, and he has been changed. Even his passing shadow brings a blessing. Even his presence is good news. He walks in the light of Christ, and he casts a long shadow. It is the same shadow of the Spirit that came upon Mary when she conceived Jesus in her womb. It is now the overshadowing presence of the apostles, communicating the healing love of God. No wonder the Church is growing.

The authorities are exasperated. Peter and all who are with him are arrested and thrown into prison. But this is the God who rolls stones away, and at daybreak, Peter is found outside the bars of imprisonment teaching the people about the liberation that comes from Christ.

COLLECT

Let your merciful ears, O Lord,
be open to the prayers of your humble servants;
and that they may obtain their petitions
make them to ask such things as shall please you;
through Jesus Christ your Son our Lord,
who is alive and reigns with you,
in the unity of the Holy Spirit,
one God, now and for ever.

Psalms **76**, 79
2 Samuel 2.1-11
Acts 5.27-end

Acts 5.27-end

The apostles are brought before the council again. They have been ordered not to talk about Jesus, but they are still doing it. Peter answers: 'We must obey God rather than any human authority.'

This faith so shapes their world view and their values that the apostles no longer feel accountable to these human authorities. They even rejoice that they suffer for the sake of the gospel.

The instinct of the authorities is to crush them (and, later on, the Church does suffer terrible persecution). But, within the council, there is one voice of godly wisdom that gives the Church the breathing space it needs so that this gospel of the Spirit, enacted in the lives of the apostles, can travel further. This is the third great theme of this book: the good news of Jesus travels across the world, to gentile as well as Jew, and from Jerusalem to Rome. If this thing 'is of human origin', says Gamaliel, 'it will fail; but if it is of God, you will not be able to overthrow them – in that case you may even be found fighting against God!'

The astonishing story of the Acts of the Apostles is precisely this: God at work through the lives of ordinary men and women who have been transformed by God's forgiveness and the gift of his spirit. It is a story being continued today.

Lord of heaven and earth,
as Jesus taught his disciples to be persistent in prayer,
give us patience and courage never to lose hope,
but always to bring our prayers before you;
through Jesus Christ our Lord.

COLLECT

73

Monday 4 August

Psalms **80**, 82
2 Samuel 3.12-end
Acts 6

Acts 6

It began, as many things do in the Church, with a row. The new Christian movement had started with high ideals about justice and economic fairness, and organized its life on a strong communal basis (see Acts 5.32). As often happens in such cases, one of the groups receiving help from the communal pot felt they were not receiving their fair share.

To prevent a serious split, the Twelve came up with a swift solution. Drawing on past experience (see Numbers 11), they made a pragmatic decision. 'Our priorities are clear; we have to pray and minister the word of God. What we need is a new structure to deal with these practical problems.' (You can almost hear the management consultants talking about 'keeping focused'.) So, seven men were appointed and authorized. The Church was changing its structure, moving from a charismatic mode into an institutional one. It happens everywhere, in all human organizations; it is unavoidable. Job descriptions were drawn up, and clear lines of accountability were established. Everything seemed neat and tidy.

And then what happened? One of the newly appointed administrators, Stephen, discovered new gifts – and all the careful plans were put under stress. The rest of the story is well known. Stephen, the back-office bureaucrat, became the first Christian to die for the faith. It is right to plan, but God's plans and ours are often very different.

COLLECT

O God, you declare your almighty power
most chiefly in showing mercy and pity:
mercifully grant to us such a measure of your grace,
that we, running the way of your commandments,
may receive your gracious promises,
and be made partakers of your heavenly treasure;
through Jesus Christ your Son our Lord,
who is alive and reigns with you,
in the unity of the Holy Spirit,
one God, now and for ever.

Psalms 87, **89.1-18**
2 Samuel 5.1-12
Acts 7.1-16

Acts 7.1-16

It's frustrating when people don't answer questions directly. Stephen had been accused of saying that Jesus would destroy the temple and had altered the teachings of Moses. 'Is this true?' asked the high priest. Instead of answering yes or no, Stephen launched into a long description of the history of Israel and its relationship with God. Why didn't he answer the question?

Maybe everything he is reported to have said was a standard response made to all critics of Jesus and his followers, and Luke simply used it in Acts as a shorthand. Or perhaps Stephen really did wish to make the point that the people of Israel had frequently treated prophets with scorn and had now made the biggest mistake of all in failing to see Jesus of Nazareth as the Messiah. This was a terrible and piercing criticism of those in power; it's no wonder they threw him out and in their anger arranged to execute him. Whatever the reasons for the question not being answered, the fact remains that Stephen was killed for his beliefs. But note how Stephen imitated Christ in his final words: 'Lord, do not hold this sin against them.'

When facing derision, scorn and contempt for our beliefs, are we able to react with wholehearted forgiveness? Pray that our hearts and souls may be so filled by God that Christ-like forgiveness becomes part of our very nature.

God of glory,
the end of our searching,
help us to lay aside
all that prevents us from seeking your kingdom,
and to give all that we have
to gain the pearl beyond all price,
through our Saviour Jesus Christ.

COLLECT

Wednesday 6 August

The Transfiguration of Our Lord

Psalms 27, 150
Ecclesiasticus 48.1-10 *or*
1 Kings 19.1-16
1 John 3.1-3

1 John 3.1-3

Outside Ravenna lies the sixth-century church of St Apollinare in Classe. In the semi-dome over the altar, there is a huge and stunning mosaic; it features St Apollinaris. Above his head is a jewelled cross, at the top of which is written *ichthus*, meaning fish, an acronym for Jesus Christ, God's son, Saviour. Below the cross is written *Salus Mundi* ('Saviour of the world'). On either side of the cross are the Greek letters *alpha* and *omega* ('beginning' and 'end'), and at the centre there is a small image of Christ. Surrounding this cross are 99 stars and, on either side in the heavens, the figures of Moses and Elijah.

The jewelled cross represents Christ's glory, the stars symbolize the lost sheep for whom he searches, and the words refer to his divinity. It's a swirling mixture of text and image, colour and symbolism (three sheep look up at the cross, representing Peter, James and John), centred on the theme of transfiguration.

The story of Jesus' transfiguration is so startling that, when we come across it in the Gospels, we do not know quite what to make of it. We should not be unnerved – for, in the presence of Christ, we are met by the glory, power and welcoming beauty of God. All we can do is gaze on that beauty and whisper to God our alleluias of thanksgiving. It is enough.

COLLECT

Father in heaven,
whose Son Jesus Christ was wonderfully transfigured
before chosen witnesses upon the holy mountain,
and spoke of the exodus he would accomplish at Jerusalem:
give us strength so to hear his voice and bear our cross
that in the world to come we may see him as he is;
who is alive and reigns with you,
in the unity of the Holy Spirit,
one God, now and for ever.

Psalms 90, **92**
2 Samuel 7.1-17
Acts 7.44-53

Acts 7.44-53

No matter how beautiful or holy our churches may be, they can never be a substitute for the presence of God when he meets us in forgiveness, in the sacraments, in the love of other people, in his word or in prayer. God is far more beautiful, more holy, more loving than any of the ideas we may have of him. From time to time, just as buildings have to be abandoned because they have served their purpose, so sometimes we have to abandon our most cherished ideas about God so that he can reveal yet more of himself to us. This can be very painful and can lead to a sense of desolation.

Yet, when we let go, we find that new promises await us: a new sense of the endless expanse of God's very being. Then words fail, as though the words themselves fissure into a thousand fragments and drift away like dust. All that remains is the glory, darkness, brilliance and silence of God, where we know that Jesus, with wounded hands, comes to embrace us. The silence of our own prayer is met by the silence of the being of God. No houses of prayer, then, no churches, no temples – nothing except the presence of God in Jesus Christ. It is that to which we are called; it is that heart of eternal love that is our destiny.

O God, you declare your almighty power
most chiefly in showing mercy and pity:
mercifully grant to us such a measure of your grace,
that we, running the way of your commandments,
may receive your gracious promises,
and be made partakers of your heavenly treasure;
through Jesus Christ your Son our Lord,
who is alive and reigns with you,
in the unity of the Holy Spirit,
one God, now and for ever.

COLLECT

77

Friday 8 August

Psalms **88** (95)
2 Samuel 7.18-end
Acts 7.54 – 8.3

Acts 7.54 – 8.3

As we read this account, we are buffeted by the opposites: the grinding of teeth with fury, followed by Stephen's vision of glory; the stoning of the martyr, followed by the sound of coats being placed on the ground; the broken body of the murdered man, compared with the upright onlooker, Saul. Yet we, the readers, know that Saul will himself soon be struck by God, not with stones, but with a flashing light. The 'supremo' of persecution will become the one who is converted: the hunter will become the hunted.

For the moment, however, in these readings from the Acts of the Apostles, we are left in a bewildering place. The story has been so full of success up to this point – all those conversations, all those new converts (see Acts 5.14); yet now the miracles, the teaching, the growth of the Church are all on hold. Instead of a steady, increasing impact, the believers are subject to a fusillade of invective and violence. The serene assurance of the ascension and the vivacity of Pentecost have given way to mayhem and murder, and believers have fled Jerusalem, scattering into the hill villages of Judea and Samaria.

The dark, vehement shadow of Saul has fallen across the sunlit streets of Jerusalem. And yet, the energy of the drama compels us to read on – is this the tragic end or a new beginning?

COLLECT

O God, you declare your almighty power
most chiefly in showing mercy and pity:
mercifully grant to us such a measure of your grace,
that we, running the way of your commandments,
may receive your gracious promises,
and be made partakers of your heavenly treasure;
through Jesus Christ your Son our Lord,
who is alive and reigns with you,
in the unity of the Holy Spirit,
one God, now and for ever.

Psalms 96, **97**, 100
2 Samuel 9
Acts 8.4-25

Acts 8.4-25

The suspense is over. The camera zooms in on Philip, who had fled from Saul. We are in Samaria, where we also encounter Simon, a magician, whom some believed to be the living embodiment of God's power. He became captivated by the message that Philip brought and was baptized. Success re-enters the story, but so does a message: the gift of God's Holy Spirit cannot be bought. Simon had thought that he could buy God's gift, but Peter denounced such an idea, angrily: 'Your money can go with you to damnation.' It is clear that while Philip had had some success as an evangelist, his converts needed correction and teaching, and Peter, having been sent with John from Jerusalem, provided it. What was at stake was the authenticity of the Christian message.

The battle for what is authentic, of course, never stops. Christians continue to debate with each other about what Jesus taught; it is unending. But there is something remarkably encouraging about this kind of dispute; it's as though God continues to wrestle with us. We are not handed a set of doctrinal statements by God, which we then have to learn and abide by; rather, he gives us his very self and, in the wrestling of that relationship, enables us to struggle towards what is true and authentic. The struggle is never over – but in it, and by it, we are blessed.

God of glory,
the end of our searching,
help us to lay aside
all that prevents us from seeking your kingdom,
and to give all that we have
to gain the pearl beyond all price,
through our Saviour Jesus Christ.

COLLECT

Monday 11 August

Acts 8.26-end

We begin with angels, always a good place to start, and end our reading with a disappearance – all very curious.

Philip was a 'seer': one who glimpsed angels, one who felt impelled to move on. Not for him the power of Jerusalem, but instead the restlessness of the long-distance traveller. He set out on the desert road and there, by chance, met an international diplomat, representing the royal court of Ethiopia. He was reading a passage from Isaiah, chapter 53, about the suffering servant, and was deeply puzzled about its meaning. Philip, invited to join him, explained that the passage referred to Jesus of Nazareth, and such were Philip's advocacy and teaching skills that the courtier asked to be baptized immediately.

And there, this gem of a story stops. Philip, like Elijah, disappears, and the Ethiopian has to make his own way home. We do not know what might have happened next. Did the diplomat take the Christian message back to Ethiopia? And what of Philip? Whom did he tell about his encounter? And what was the impact of the telling?

For many of us, it is also true that an apparently casual conversation with a stranger can cause our lives to change. Looking back on such events, what seemed casual takes on the appearance of an epiphany: a moment when the angel of God reveals to us the Most High ...

COLLECT

Almighty and everlasting God,
you are always more ready to hear than we to pray
and to give more than either we desire or deserve:
pour down upon us the abundance of your mercy,
forgiving us those things of which our conscience is afraid
and giving us those good things which we are not worthy to
     ask
but through the merits and mediation
of Jesus Christ your Son our Lord,
who is alive and reigns with you,
in the unity of the Holy Spirit,
one God, now and for ever.

Psalms **106*** (or 103)
2 Samuel 12.1-25
Acts 9.1-19a

Acts 9.1-19a

Saul now returns to the story in an episode that has shaped accounts of conversion ever since. He is still breathing murderous threats against Jesus' disciples. While travelling to Damascus, he is smitten by God's power and falls to the ground. The voice calls, and Saul, with a giveaway response, asks: 'Who are you, Lord?'

The diplomat sought God in the Scriptures and had his eyes opened to the beauties of Christ as the suffering servant. Saul is blinded by the inner conviction of the truth that the risen Jesus is within his followers. In killing Stephen, he has tried to kill the Christ.

Is it any wonder, then, that he, the terrible, vengeful judge, has to be led, stumbling and scuffing, and completely overwhelmed, into Damascus? There, he hears words of enormous grace; an unknown man calls him 'brother' and promises that not only will he see again, he will also be filled with the Holy Spirit. It is enough. Paul is baptized. There is no turning back. The truth of God has pierced him to the quick, and the zeal that drove him to destroy will become the zeal of mission.

It takes much courage and humility to pray, daily, 'Tell me, Lord, who you are' – but it is a prayer each of us needs to utter if we are to discover what God wants us to do and be.

God of constant mercy,
who sent your Son to save us:
remind us of your goodness,
increase your grace within us,
that our thankfulness may grow,
through Jesus Christ our Lord.

COLLECT

81

Wednesday 13 August

Psalms 110, 111, 112
2 Samuel 15.1-12
Acts 9.19b-31

Acts 9.19b-31

There's no point in beating about the bush: we have a problem here. When Paul wrote to the Galatians about his conversion, he explained that immediately afterwards he went to Arabia and only later returned to Damascus. He clearly states that he did not then go up to Jerusalem (see Galatians 1.13-20), but waited three years before doing so. However, Luke says that Paul stayed in Damascus for some time. It's a puzzle; perhaps Luke compressed the timescale to create a greater sense of urgency. But it is clear that Paul's wiry energy soon got him into trouble and he had to make a dramatic escape from Damascus after stirring up discontent. In Jerusalem, he remained troublesome, and soon, fearing for his life, Paul was escorted to Caesarea and sent home to Tarsus.

It would be fascinating to know what the disciples said to one another as they waved him aboard his ship. Were they relieved that such a turbulent, charismatic firebrand was now someone else's problem? Or were they remorseful about their initial lack of trust in such a remarkable theological street fighter?

In spite of Luke trying to give coherent shape to these early days of the Church, you sense that everything was, in fact, in a state of continuous change. The explosive truths of Jesus' death and resurrection are necessarily disruptive – eternity and God's love cannot be contained or controlled.

COLLECT

Almighty and everlasting God,
you are always more ready to hear than we to pray
and to give more than either we desire or deserve:
pour down upon us the abundance of your mercy,
forgiving us those things of which our conscience is afraid
and giving us those good things which we are not worthy to
    ask
but through the merits and mediation
of Jesus Christ your Son our Lord,
who is alive and reigns with you,
in the unity of the Holy Spirit,

Psalms 113, **115**
2 Samuel 15.13-end
Acts 9.32-end

Acts 9.32-end

After the turbulence of Paul, we enter calmer waters, in the company of Peter. He travels, like an early bishop, to see his flock – and goes to Lydda and Joppa. In Lydda, he heals a bedridden man; in Joppa, he restores Tabitha to life. Thus he continues the work of healing and teaching that Jesus himself had carried out in his own lifetime. Substitute the name 'Jesus' for the name 'Peter' in either of these stories, and you could be back in Luke's Gospel.

In reading the Acts, however, we can see Luke constructing the story with care. Turbulence is followed by calm, but there is also a sense that something dramatic may yet happen. In this episode, we are lulled into a sense of relief that the apostles' pastoral and teaching ministry is going well, but the story ends: 'Peter stayed on at Joppa for some time at the house of a tanner called Simon.' Why has Luke mentioned this? What is about to happen? Are we going to encounter more change, more turbulence?

The skill of Luke is that as a storyteller, he relates his stories to our own human experience. There are times of calm in our lives and times of extreme uncertainty; that is simply how life is. And, within both the calm and the turbulence, says Luke, there is the movement of the Spirit of God.

God of constant mercy,
who sent your Son to save us:
remind us of your goodness,
increase your grace within us,
that our thankfulness may grow,
through Jesus Christ our Lord.

COLLECT

Friday 15 August

The Blessed Virgin Mary

Psalms 98, 138, 147.1-12
Isaiah 7.10-15
Luke 11.27,28

Luke 11.27,28

No one actually knows when Mary, the mother of our Lord, died – or where she died. Some legends claim she died in Jerusalem, and others in Ephesus. One of the legends tells how an angel came to tell Mary that in three days she would be assumed into heaven to be with her son. John and all the disciples were whisked up by clouds and taken to Mary's house so they could be present when she died. At her death, her body was surrounded by red roses, symbolizing the martyrs, and by lilies of the valley, signifying angels, virgins and confessors.

The stories are glorious in their innocence and complexity, striving to convey the sense of awe and gratitude that any believer must feel for all that Mary did and gave towards the salvation of humankind, through the birth and life of her son, Jesus.

In the Roman Catholic Church, 15 August is known as the 'Assumption of the Blessed Virgin Mary', and in the Eastern Church the feast is called the 'Dormition of the Virgin'. Whatever language is used to try to define Mary's feast day, what is clear is that her love and suffering are a profound part of the Christian salvation story.

On this day, bring to mind all the gifts of motherhood you have witnessed and known, and then simply give thanks for Mary, mother of our Lord.

COLLECT

Almighty God,
who looked upon the lowliness of the Blessed Virgin Mary
and chose her to be the mother of your only Son:
grant that we who are redeemed by his blood
may share with her in the glory of your eternal kingdom;
through Jesus Christ your Son our Lord,
who is alive and reigns with you,
in the unity of the Holy Spirit,
one God, now and for ever.

Psalms 120, **121**, 122
2 Samuel 17.1-23
Acts 10.17-33

Saturday 16 August

Acts 10.17-33

It's important not to begin part-way through the story, so let us return to the very first verse of Acts 10 and read the story all the way through to the end of the chapter, then turn to verse 17 and read through until verse 33.

At the heart of this story is yet another encounter: Peter, confronted by a senior soldier in the Roman army. The centurion has a vision in which he is asked to arrange to meet Simon Peter. Meanwhile, Peter has had a vision in which all his previous religious convictions are challenged. Both men are challenged to change. In honesty they meet, Peter explaining that as a Jew he has to obey certain rules governing such a meeting; the centurion, used to commanding, abases himself in front of a man whose land he and his army are occupying. Peter tells him to stand up, and, on the basis of their openness to each other and to God, another breakthrough in the life of the Church occurs, a breakthrough that was to have momentous consequences.

Sharing our common humanity with those who are different from ourselves is always uncertain – will games of power be played? But when true meeting happens, the release of energy and creative newness is wonderful. Pray for the courage to trust your own and other people's humanity, and wait upon God for the consequences.

Almighty and everlasting God,
you are always more ready to hear than we to pray
and to give more than either we desire or deserve:
pour down upon us the abundance of your mercy,
forgiving us those things of which our conscience is afraid
and giving us those good things which we are not worthy to ask
but through the merits and mediation
of Jesus Christ your Son our Lord,
who is alive and reigns with you,
in the unity of the Holy Spirit,

COLLECT

85

Book 4
Reflections for Daily Prayer:
Trinity 13 to Christ the King
Publication date: July 2008

Contributors: John Pritchard, Jane Williams, Tom Smail,
Emma Ineson, Maggi Dawn, Alan Garrow, Ian Paul

£3.99 978 0 7151 4159 5
Reflections for Daily Prayer is published four times a year
– October, January, April and July – and is available from
all good Christian bookshops. You can also obtain it
direct from the publishers (see page 88).

Common Worship: Daily Prayer

Daily Prayer is ideal for anyone
wanting to follow a regular pattern
of prayer, praise and Bible-reading.
The material may be used in small
groups or individually.

£20.00 (Hardback)
978 0 7151 2073 6
202 x 125mm, 896 pages

Time to Pray

Compact, soft-case volume offers a user-friendly
resource for praying through the week.
The simple, accessible structure
allows even those with little time
on their hands the opportunity to
'recharge' for a few minutes
each day. Includes Prayer During
the Day (for every single day of
the week), Night Prayer and
selected psalms from *Common
Worship: Daily Prayer*. To be used
by individuals or small groups.

£12.99 (Soft case)
978 0 7151 2122 7
199 x 125mm, 112 pages

What others say about *Reflections for Daily Prayer*

'Simple yet often profound, attractively presented and easy to use, *Reflections* is a real aid to "going deeper" with the lectionary readings.'

Revd Jan McFarlane, Bishop's Chaplain and Diocesan Director of Communications, Diocese of Norwich

'With its mixture of authors from a wide range of specialisms, the book will be a helpful resource for anyone who is keen to spend devotional time with God during the day, and its pocket size will make it particularly handy for commuters.'

The Church of England Newspaper

'This is an ideal book to use with Morning Prayer or Prayer During the Day.'

Praxis News of Worship

What do you think of *Reflections for Daily Prayer*? We'd love to hear from you – simply email us on **publishing@c-of-e.org.uk** or write to us at Church House Publishing, Church House, Great Smith Street, London SW1P 3AZ.

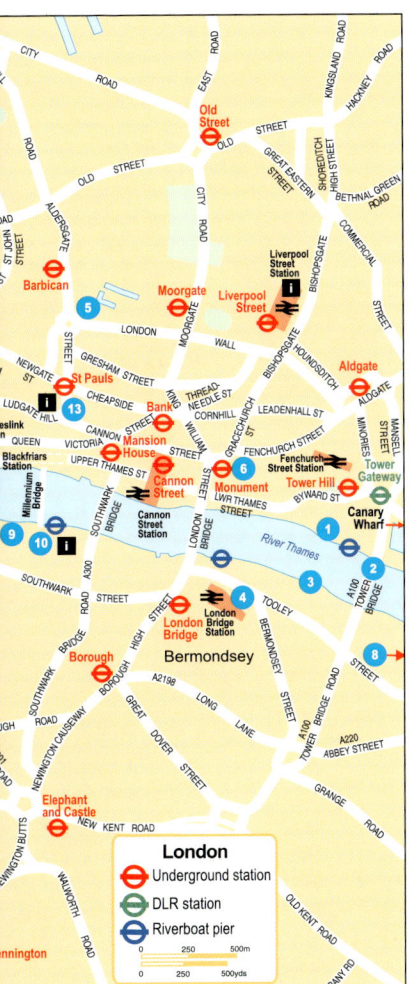

MAP KEY

1 Tower of London
2 Tower Bridge
3 HMS *Belfast*
4 The London Dungeon
5 Museum of London
6 The Monument
7 Somerset House
8 Greenwich
9 Tate Modern
10 Shakespeare's Globe
11 Imperial War Museum
12 London Eye and the South Bank
13 St Paul's Cathedral
14 Trafalgar Square
15 National Gallery
16 National Portrait Gallery
17 Horse Guards
18 Downing Street
19 Churchill War Rooms
20 Houses of Parliament
21 Buckingham Palace and
   The Queen's Gallery
22 Royal Mews
23 Changing the Guard
24 Westminster Abbey
25 Westminster Cathedral
26 Tate Britain
27 Piccadilly Circus
28 Sherlock Holmes Museum
29 Covent Garden
30 London Transport Museum
31 British Museum
32 Madame Tussauds
33 The Royal Parks
34 London Zoo
35 Harrods
36 Science Museum
37 Natural History Museum
38 Victoria and Albert Museum
39 Kensington Palace
40 Notting Hill

ROYAL CONNECTIONS

● Buckingham Palace

Looking every inch a royal palace, this has been the London residence of the British monarch since Queen Victoria moved in, in 1837. Buckingham Palace is owned by the State, unlike Sandringham and Balmoral which belong to the Royal Family. At times of national crisis and great state events, Buckingham Palace – at the head of The Mall – is a focal point for the British people. The ornate suite of rooms known as the State Apartments, used for ceremonial occasions, is open to the public every summer. The Queen's Gallery at Buckingham Palace, where you can see works of art from the Royal Collection, is open daily. The Queen lives in the north wing and you'll see the Royal Standard fluttering overhead when she is in residence. The 16-hectare (40-acre) park-like garden is where she hosts her annual garden parties. *www.royal.gov.uk*